Turning Points

Very Important!

Pg. 75 (at bottom) + continued on pg. 76. RAB
6/17/2000

Turning Points

Moments of Grace,
Steps toward Wholeness

Myrlene L. J. Hamilton

Judson Press ® Valley Forge

Turning Points: Moments of Grace, Steps toward Wholeness
© 1997 Judson Press, Valley Forge, PA 19482-0851

Unless otherwise indicated, Bible quotations in this volume are from the New Revised Standard Version of the Bible (NRSV), copyright © 1989 by the Division of Christian Education of the National Council of the Churches of Christ in the United States of America. Used by permission. All rights reserved.

Text illustrations are used by permission of the artist, Jeanne Buoncristiano.

Library of Congress Cataloging-in-Publication Data
Hamilton, Myrlene L. J., 1952-
  Turning points : moments of grace, steps toward wholeness / Myrlene L.J. Hamilton.
    p. cm.
  Includes bibliographical references.
  ISBN 0-8170-1259-1 (alk. paper)
  1. Suffering—Religious aspects—Christianity. 2. Life change events—Religious aspects—Christianity. 3. Grace (Theology)
  I. Title.
  BV4909.H36 1997
  248.8'6—dc21   96-39623

Printed in the U.S.A.
05 04 03 02 01 00 99 98 97
10 9 8 7 6 5 4 3 2 1

To
Kim Birdwell,
Ed Gee,
and
my family

Contents

Preface

Several years ago I was asked to speak at a weekend retreat on the topic "Give Thanks." While I was eager to do it, I wondered how I was going to fill up four major talks on the subject of giving thanks. Not that I hadn't given any number of sermons on giving thanks before, but they were all pretty much the same. I was accustomed to preaching an annual sermon on the topic, always around "Thanksgiving" time. But as I studied and prayed and prepared, I made some new discoveries about the nature of thanksgiving as it relates to our relationship with God. I was particularly moved by the rediscovery of the Greek word *eucharisteo,* which means "to give thanks" and whose English counterpart—Eucharist—is a synonym for the Lord's Supper. The study led me below the surface of "thanksgiving" to the place where God's grace intersects with life's struggles. What I learned about myself, about God, and about the power of thankful living touched me deeply.

In the intervening years, the thoughts at the heart of this book have percolated through my experiences and observations of the church and of people in general. Most recently they have become interwoven with an awareness of how pervasive addiction is in our society and in the church as well.

The lives of people today are filled to the brim with pressure, demands, stress, goals, and activities. Yet so many lives are lacking in fulfillment, peace, and joy. So many people have lives, jobs, and relationships that are constantly on the verge of breaking from the strain of trying to fill their cup with drink that does not satisfy but keeps them coming back for more, just the same. These are the people who need to know Christ and need the fellowship of the church. Yet when I look at the church whose call it is to reach out with Christ's healing love, I see a mirror image of the overly busy, stressed out, addicted world that we seek to serve.

If we in the church are not ourselves being renewed—not "in recovery," to use the language of addiction—how can we possibly bring hope and healing to others who need it?

I want people to know the touch of God and to rejoice in their relationships with God's people. My heart's desire in writing this book is to encourage Christians to be honest about where they are in life—to acknowledge struggle, pain, and sin; to learn to turn to God in all of life's struggles; and to experience God's healing and revitalization. I believe the result of such a turning will be Christians who are open and responsive to the movement of God— Christians who are empowered to reach out to a world that is desperate for Good News.

Acknowledgments

The Women's Retreat Committee of Christ Community Church, Sacramento, California, planted the first seed thoughts that eventually grew into this book when they invited me to address its 1991 retreat on the topic of "Give Thanks." The Women's Retreat Committee of Bidwell Memorial Presbyterian Church in Chico, California, enabled me to further develop these thoughts at a subsequent retreat that they held. I want to thank both of these groups for their warm response to the messages that I shared with them.

Kim Birdwell and Ed Gee, whose stories appear in this book, are two people whose faith and courage inspire me. I am grateful for their friendship and for the privilege of being involved in extraordinary turning points in their journeys.

Special appreciation goes to the following people who gave helpful critiques of this manuscript: my colleague and friend, the Reverend Connie Dorn; and members of my family: my mother, Elsie Jacobson; my brother, Dr. Allan Jacobson; my sisters, Janet Peterson and Karen Kinder; and my husband, Ed.

I am grateful to the editorial staff at Judson Press for their professional assistance, along with their friendly working style.

I also want to thank the people of Morning Star Presbyterian Church, who have helped me in this project more than they know. Their laughter, their openness, and their support have created an atmosphere of freedom that allows me to be myself and challenges me to do my best. Their willingness to make recovery a priority in their ministry and in their own lives has also been a great source of encouragement in the writing of this book.

PART ONE
Learning to Turn

CHAPTER 1

Time to Turn

For the most part, time seems to beat a steady rhythm in the background of our daily activities. We get up each morning, attend to the day's tasks, and finally go to bed at night, following routines familiar and oft repeated. But for all of us there are moments when the passage of time takes on a new dimension. Time may even seem to stand still in the face of a particular event. The time is made special or significant by what happens in it. A baby is born. Someone dies. We get a promotion. We lose a job. We fall in love. We hear God's voice. We fall into temptation and sin. We are faced with a decision. We experience great disaster.

We commemorate such times with a bouquet of flowers, a phone call, family gatherings, a pilgrimage to a cemetery. . . . Indeed, some moments are different, unique, life changing.

One Moment in Time

For my friend Kim, such a moment struck on her thirtieth birthday. Though she recognized this birthday as an important milestone, she planned nothing extraordinary beyond her usual dinner out with her husband, Barry, and their son, Bryan, along with their extended family. But discovering a lump in her breast froze the moment in time. Despite all the odds in her favor, the lump turned out to be an invasive carcinoma. Cancer. Surgery—a radical mastectomy—revealed that the cancer had spread to her lymph system. Kim's odds of survival were slim. And even if she did survive, life could never be the same after her thirtieth birthday.

In the New Testament there are two different words that describe the movement of time. One is *chronos,* from which we get our words "chronology" and "chronological." *Chronos* refers to what we usually mean when we say "time"—the constant ticking of a clock as the days go by. The other biblical word, *kairos* (pronounced with a long *i,* as in "Cairo"), is used for those unique moments that have a profound effect that goes well beyond the "moment." For instance, in Acts 1:6-7 Jesus refers to "times" and "seasons" (RSV) that have been established by God. While the "times" (*chronos*) reflect the movement of history, the "seasons" (*kairos*) are the "joints or articulations in these times, the critical epoch-making periods fore-ordained of God."[1] The Bible is of course full of such *kairos* moments, since the Bible is about God's intervention in history.

The day had begun like any other day for Simeon. As was his custom, he went to the temple to pray the same prayer he always prayed, asking God to allow him to see the Messiah before he died. He felt in his heart that God's answer was yes, yet each day went by without a glimpse or a glimmer that the Messiah had come. And he wasn't getting any younger. Anna, an eighty-four-year-old prophet who practically lived in the temple, was in prayer that morning as well. Her prayer was that God would grant a new vision for the future of God's people.

Simeon saw them first, this young couple with a newborn in their arms. His pulse quickened as he walked over to greet them. By this time, Mary was getting used to strangers taking an interest in her son. She smiled and turned back the blanket so Simeon could see him. One look into the infant's eyes made the old man's heart ache for joy. Simeon then took the baby in his arms. "Now I can die in peace," he said. "I have seen the Lord's Messiah." Hearing the commotion, Anna joined the little group. A shiver of excitement coursed up and down her spine, as she, too, recognized her Lord. "Praise God!" she said in a loud voice. Then she began to preach about the child to all who were waiting for God's salvation to come. (See Luke 2:25-38.)

The biblical *kairos* moments are epoch making, not just for those who experienced them, but for all the world: Adam and Eve's sin, the Great Flood, the Exodus, the Crucifixion and Resurrection, Pentecost. Even events that were very personal—the call of Abraham, David's sin with Bathsheba, Rahab's kindness to two Hebrew spies, Paul's conversion—affect us all, not just as examples but because they are a part of the fabric of the history of the people of God. In one way or another, these people entered into the movement of the Holy Spirit, thus leading the people of God to the present moment.

But *kairos* moments are not just for the Bible. They are not limited to events that will affect the course of world history or the history of God's people. Like Kim, all of us have *kairos* moments in our own lives. We speak of "critical moments" or the "nick of time." My husband, who is a volunteer police chaplain, sometimes gets called out on "critical incidents." These are the tragic events—hostage situations, accidents with multiple deaths, suicides, etc.—that not only affect the victims but also profoundly impact those who respond to them. Ed is there to minister to the victims and to the officers who are traumatized by what they have experienced. There have been many moments in which my life was changed forever, for good or for ill: the day my father died, the day I met my husband, the day I started seminary. For Kim, it was the day she found a lump.

Kairos moments do not occur at our convenience. While some may be the fruit of our own actions or decisions, these moments are most often thrust upon us by circumstance or by the whims of other people or by the sovereign grace of God. Even so, within each *kairos* experience there is something of our choosing—there is a choice to be made. Whether the event itself is positive or negative, the choice we have within the moment is to move either toward God in thanksgiving or away from God in bitterness or self-absorption. If *kairos* moments are joints in the bones of time, then they have significant impact on the direction our lives will take. They are moments of turning one way or another.

To make the most of a *kairos* moment, stated simply, is to learn to turn. Turn to God. In everything.

Turning Point

Another Greek word used by the writers of the New Testament is significant here. The word is *metanoia,* and we translate it "repentance." The verb form literally means "to turn or return" and suggests that those who have once strayed from God (or who never knew God in the first place) turned to God. "More than a mere change of mind, though it includes this; it represents a reorientation of one's whole life and personality."[2] *Metanoia* is used to describe the event we call conversion—the reorientation of life to become a follower of Jesus Christ.

By occupation, Andrew was a fisherman. In his heart he was a seeker. Like many of his contemporaries, Andrew had a deep conviction that the world was standing on the brink of something big. The coming of the Messiah was near. When a firebrand called John the Baptist began preaching a message of repentance, urging people to prepare their hearts for the Messiah's arrival, Andrew felt even more sure of his conviction. He became a devoted follower of John so that he wouldn't miss a thing. The day came when John baptized Jesus in the Jordan River. When Andrew heard John refer to him as "the Lamb of God" and "the Son of God," Andrew turned from John and from his fishing and began following Jesus. It was the turning point that John's ministry had prepared him for. His life would never be the same because his life was reoriented to a new priority: following Jesus. He would still go fishing from time to time, but fishing would no longer be his primary vocation.

A more contemporary example of *metanoia* is my friend Kim, who in her *kairos* moment faced death and found faith. When she addressed the reality of her cancer, Kim, who had not been a churchgoer prior to that, began to seek God. She started to attend church on Sundays and brought most of her family with her. Often during the week she would return to the sanctuary to pray. In the midst of her intense battle for life, she reached out to God and found that God was there. One day she came down the hall to my study after her time of prayer in the sanctuary and told me the story of her cancer and her newfound commitment. "With what God has done for me," Kim says about her *metanoia,* "I could never live my life the same as before, since I see so many choices now. My life was happy before I got cancer, but now my life has purpose. Now I want to tell my story to everyone who will listen because I want people to know that no matter how tough things get, there is hope."

But *metanoia* is not just a once-for-all experience. It also applies to other turning points described in this book. For God's people, all of life is a turning toward God. The Old Testament tells a dramatic story about a young Hebrew woman named Esther, who faced a *kairos* moment of gargantuan proportions. Exiled from her homeland, Judea, she (along with most Jews) lived in Persia. Her beauty won the heart of the Persian king, Xerxes, and she became his queen. But she kept her Jewish heritage a secret. Esther lived in a secular environment in which God's name was not even mentioned. Yet God was active in her life and in the life of the exiled Jewish community.

Closeted away in Xerxes' harem, Esther was oblivious to the political intrigue swirling around her. A wicked man named Haman, who hated Jews, became "most favored" by Xerxes. He convinced the king to set a "lucky day" when all the Jews would be annihilated. Upon learning of this decree, the Jews went into mourning—all except Esther, who knew nothing about it. Esther's uncle, Mordecai, tore his clothes, covered himself with sackcloth and ashes, and wailing at the top of his lungs throughout the city, he stopped at the king's gate. When Esther heard about her uncle, she sent him some clean clothes, which he refused. Then she sent a servant to find out what was going on. Mordecai informed her about everything. Then he challenged her to go to the king and seek mercy for her people. Esther sent back a message reminding Mordecai that no one, not even the queen, was permitted to initiate a conversation with the king. Anyone who dared to approach the king was executed, with one exception. If the king raised his golden scepter, the person was spared.

Esther added a postscript to her message. "It's been more than a month since the king has sent for me." Mordecai replied, "Do not think that in the king's palace you will escape any more than all the other Jews. For if you keep silence at such a time as this, relief and deliverance will rise for the Jews from another quarter, but you and your father's family will perish. Who knows? Perhaps you have come to royal dignity for just such a time as this" (Esther 4:13b-14). Esther could not have known what a significant moment this was—how things would have changed if Haman's plan to annihilate the Jews had been carried out. But she did recognize that it was a turning point for her and for those she loved. She had to decide whether to remain in her protective cocoon or to stick her neck out. She chose to risk her life by going to the king. As it happened, the king raised his golden scepter, and in the end the Jews were saved.

The New Testament mentions a young man named John Mark, who had trouble keeping his Christian life on track. He accompanied Paul and Barnabas on their missionary journey, but when they got to Perga in Pamphylia, he left them abruptly to return to Jerusalem. No reason is given. Perhaps he was homesick or seasick. Perhaps he was tired of the ministry or was afraid of the dangers the missionaries faced. Maybe he was just irresponsible. Later, when Paul and Barnabas made plans to return to some of the churches that they started, Barnabas wanted to take Mark along again. Paul refused to take someone who had deserted previously. (See Acts 13:13 and 15:36-40.) The disagreement between Paul and Barnabas became so heated that the two parted company. Paul took Silas, while Barnabas took Mark. The first step in his journey with Barnabas was, by all accounts, the beginning of a major turning point for Mark. Certainly Barnabas, whose name means "son of encouragement" and whose encouraging ways had influenced many, including Paul, had a great deal of influence on him. Later Mark even won back the respect of Paul. Writing to the church at Colossae, Paul said, "Aristarchus my fellow prisoner greets you, as does Mark the cousin of Barnabas, concerning whom you have received instructions—if he comes to you, welcome him" (Colossians 4:10). Later he asks Timothy to bring Mark, "for he is very useful in serving me" (2 Timothy 4:11). In addition, Mark is credited with writing the Gospel that bears his name.

Those of us who were glued to our TV screens as Neil Armstrong stepped out of the space capsule onto the surface of the moon will never forget hearing him say that it was "one small step for a man, one giant leap for mankind." Such is the nature of many turning points. The physical movement may be slight, but the ultimate impact of it can hardly be measured. Four fishermen took a few steps off their boats, dropped their nets, and followed a man who said, "I want you to fish for people." These same people were later referred to as having turned the world upside down (Acts 17:6). In the fall of 1980 a man, having battled intense personal pain for several years, walked cautiously through the door of a small church. Two women greeters took him by the hand and sat him down between them in the folding chairs in the back row. "You're just going to love our new little woman pastor," they said. He did. For him—and for me—it was an important turning point. Had I overheard their refererence to a "little woman pastor," I might have had words with those two dear women. The point is that such steps are life changing, not because of their size, but because they are decisive.

Change

When we talk about *kairos* and *metanoia,* we are talking about change, of course. Turning points are the stuff of which change is made—not only the changes that are thrust on us by circumstances or by the will of others but also the inward change that can move us Godward in any circumstance.

Change is no stranger to those of us who live on the brink of the twenty-first century. It is thrust upon us all the time. In spite of the familiarity of change, it is not always our friend. Most of us do not welcome it, do not trust it, do not feel comfortable around it. In fact, we work very hard to make our environment impervious to it.

Eugenia Gamble says,

> In that quiet place in our hearts, change has come to be associated with loss, dissolution, regression, and aban-donment. Change has become a threat to the fabric of safety that we have woven: in terms of what our church, our family, even we ourselves, should look like, sound like, and do. . . . When we are faced with change, the institutions, people, or programs involved become sacred symbols of what life should be, and we cling to them.[3]

Our fear of change often reveals more about our inner struggles than we might be willing to admit. On my eighteenth birthday, I was disturbed to hear the ka-chunk, ka-chunk of an ax against the trunk of a tree. I instantly realized what was happening. My dad was chopping down a tree that I had literally "grown up with." Our old prairie farmhouse had two front porches, one on the ground floor and another stacked above it. The tree was an interloper that had grown up smack against the porches. Its roots were threatening the foundation of the house. From time to time my parents talked about chopping it down. Though all of us knew that the tree didn't belong there, somehow it had become a part of the family. My brother, my two sisters, and I had all climbed up in its branches at one time or another. But on my eighteenth birthday, my dad decided it had to come down. I went outside and pleaded with him to let the tree live. I couldn't bear to see it go, in spite of the threat it posed to the house. For whatever reason, my dad listened to my plea and stopped chopping the tree.

Looking back, I realize that my overzealous concern for the tree had deeper roots than the tree itself. I was aware that something was chopping away at my dad's health, though at the time, I did not know what. Instinctively, though, I knew that it threatened the foundation of my life. I was scared to death. Scared *of* death. As it turned out, my father was dying. While the atmosphere smelled of change, I hung on for dear life to all that was familiar, including the tree that grew up on the north side of our house.

Home

While we may flail against outward change, we are called to embrace a more important change. *Kairos* moments are key moments for us. If we let them, they will lead us home. Although I didn't know it at the time my dad was growing wheat on our farm in South Dakota, I recently learned that the roots of wheat go down at least seven feet into the soil. My roots grew deep into that South Dakota soil, too, and for eighteen years, home was my source of security, my stability, my anchor.

That farmhouse sits vacant and crumbling now. My family still owns it, but no one lives there. In the years that have passed since my eighteenth birthday, I have called more than twenty places "home" in seven states. My years as a nomad have forced me to examine what I mean when I say "home" and where my roots really are—what it is that gives me security and stability. Those years have led me to discover a home that is not bound by geography and is not dependent on things staying the same. I was a Christian long before my eighteenth birthday, but in the intervening years there have been many *kairos* moments, many choices, many turnings—sometimes in wrong directions but overall in a course that leads to the city that has foundations (Hebrews 11:10), whose builder and maker is God.

C. S. Lewis, in his book *The Problem of Pain*, makes a statement that has been comforting to me in many of my own personal turning points:

The settled happiness and security which we all desire, God withholds from us by the very nature of the world; but joy, pleasure, and merriment He has scattered broadcast. We are never safe, but we have plenty of fun, and some ecstasy. It is not hard to see why. The security we crave would teach us to rest our hearts in this world and pose an obstacle to our return to God. . . . Our Father refreshes us on the journey with some pleasant inns, but will not encourage us to mistake them for home.[4]

We find the same message in the Bible in many places, most poetically, I think, in Psalm 90: "Lord, you have been our dwelling place in all generations" (v. 1). God, you are home.

Refocusing

No matter how many times we turn to God, the temptation is always there to turn away. The world is filled with distractions large and small. It becomes a matter of focus. Learning to turn begins with how we look at our world. Before we can turn, most of us need to refocus.

My all-time favorite sport is tennis. After I broke my leg a couple of years back, I temporarily hung up my racquet. But even if I never play another set, I won't forget the cardinal rule of tennis: Keep your eye on the ball. There are lots of techniques and fine points to learn about the game of tennis. But nothing is more crucial to the game than that one simple rule. You stop watching the ball and your game goes to pot, no matter how many other techniques you may know.

The Christian life has a cardinal rule too. "You shall love the LORD your God with all your heart" (Deuteronomy 6:5). No matter what other life skills we may develop, no matter what other information we may acquire, this remains our most basic task—to love God with all that we have and all that we are, and to let this love spill over into our relationships with other people. It is easy to lose this focus, to take our minds and hearts away from the love of God, especially during *kairos* moments. Because they are often so intense and so dramatic, we can get absorbed in these moments themselves or in our fear or in our pain, whatever a particular event evokes. Often we turn inward and become introspective to such a degree that we lose our perspective. We forget the love God has for us, forget to focus our own love on God. The task then becomes to refocus, to realign our life with God. To re-turn.

To do this, we need to recover our sense of awe for who God is and for how much God loves us. I remember clear, dark summer nights back on the farm in South Dakota—looking up at the Milky Way, trying to even imagine how big a number you would have to create in order to say how many stars there were. And I remember riding a very fast elevator to the observation deck of the Empire State Building and and seeing traffic from that perspective for the first time. I remember thinking that if two cars were to collide way down there, and I chanced to see it, I would feel very distant and detached from it. Certainly my small collisions with life must look awfully small to a God who created so many stars and planets. And yet, awesome as it sounds, God has the hairs on my head numbered and God cares when I am hurting.

What could be more awesome than that? The God who created the universe cares about me and cares about you. The God who created the universe took the form of a little baby who grew up to be an adult who died on a cross for you and for me. This same God cares about us in the midst of every life-altering experience that life dishes out.

We need to change our perspective.

Each turning—each re-turning—to God has its own distinctive characteristics. Sometimes it feels like turning an ocean liner in a crowded harbor or like turning a Mack truck in quicksand. Other times we are like ballet dancers, so lifted by the Spirit's presence that we turn with grace and ease. Each time, each turning is different, unique as a snowflake, yet together they create a pattern that is our life. And each time, whether difficult or easy, the turning is made possible by the knowledge that the One to whom we turn is both safe harbor and grand choreographer.

Interlude: Crane Prairie

When my husband and I were vacationing in central Oregon a few years ago, we spent a couple of very long days fishing at Crane Prairie Reservoir. Dead trees stick their necks high above the water all over the lake as monuments to its sylvan past and hazards to boaters. This lake is touted to be one of the best trout fisheries in the area. The preferred method for trout fishing at

Crane Prairie is to tie up to one of the snags out in the middle of the lake, put a live dragonfly nymph (the locals just call them "bugs") on your hook, tie on a bobber—anathema to a dyed-in-the-wool fly fisherman like Ed—toss the thing into the water, and wait. When in Rome, we thought . . .

We sat wordlessly in our boat, tied up to a snag, staring at the red-and-white bobbers that refused to bob. As the sun shone brighter and brighter, our mood became darker and darker. We continued to watch the inactive bobbers as the hours passed. We became bored and more than a little disgruntled.

From time to time one or the other of us would look up and take in the beauty of the place: regal osprey sitting high above the water in their nests, bald eagles swooping down to scoop a fish out of the water (notably more successful than we), the noisy cormorants using the lake as a runway: splashing their wings in the water and then whistling in the air as they called to one another in their amusing throaty voices. And the lake itself: a mirror reflecting Mounts Bachelor, Brokentop, and South Sister, along with the surrealistic dead trees, standing like guardians over the mythical schools of trout living in their shadows.

Sometimes when I looked up, away from the motionless bobbers, a verse came into my mind: "O LORD, our LORD, how majestic is thy name in all the earth!" (Psalm 8:1 RSV). Looking up the psalm later, I was reminded that it continues, "When I look at thy heavens, the work of thy fingers, the moon and the stars which thou hast established; what is man that thou art mindful of him, and the son of man that thou dost care for him?" (v. 3). A good lesson to take to heart on a day of unsuccessful fishing—or on any other day.

How often it is that we continue to look down, staring at the source of our discouragement. If we look up, we may be amazed at the beauty and the grace in our world. If we look up, we may rediscover God's amazing love for us.

CHAPTER 2

Firm Footing

After a recent heavy snowfall (twenty-four inches in as many hours!), I was taking our three Labradors down a wooded path—a walk that is usually brisk and easy but now was impeded by the dog-deep snow. In my own experience on the Jersey shore, snowfall usually amounted to a dusting of snow or a bit of freezing rain, maybe a couple of inches. Two feet is rare, to say the least, so the dogs and I were not used to wading in the stuff. Buck and Spike made an easy transition, beginning to half-leap, half-swim in the pillowy snow. But our middle dog, Ramey, was obviously uncomfortable with the new terrain. Earlier snowfalls had energized her, causing her to prance and play. But this was just too much. She hesitated to walk, much less dash about with abandon. She seemed unsure of her footing. What lay beneath that thick, soft layer? There could be a bramble or a sharp rock. She just wasn't sure where her feet would land. It might as well have been quicksand. She took a few faltering steps forward and then stopped and looked at me as if to say, "Can we go in now?"

Ramey's behavior in the snow reminds me of what many of us experience when life throws a blizzard of *kairos* moments into our path. The ground is obscured, and we can't always see where to take the next step. In such a situation we are sometimes hesitant to walk in faith, much less leap, because we, like Ramey, want to be sure we are on firm footing.

Building on a Firm Foundation

Once upon a time there were two builders: one who knew his stuff and another who couldn't tell a two-by-four from a shingle. Each wanted a nice little home with an ocean view. One took the time to dig down beneath the sand to find the bedrock, and then built on that solid foundation; the other drove right down onto the beach with a pickup load of two-by-fours and began to throw together a cabin. Each one built what looked to be a respectable home. Each one also built in an area that was well known for its flash floods. And when the wind and the rain beat down, only one house remained standing. (See Matthew 7 or Luke 6 for the original version of this story.)

All of us know (many of us from hard experience) that no matter what it is we are building, the foundation is crucial. This holds true for building a career, a marriage, a church, a family. For generations this story about the two builders has provided wise advice for the people of God: build your life on the strong foundation of the Rock of Ages—Jesus Christ. And when the storms of life come, you will weather them.

The story and its message strike a chord with most of us because there is lodged in the human heart a deep desire for a sense of security—that profound and abiding sense that things are going to be OK. That we're safe no matter what storms may come. Human beings in general, and people in our modern Western culture in particular, tend to prefer the kind of security provided by things that we can see and feel, things that we can hear and smell. Things that we can measure and weigh or put under a microscope and examine. We like the feel of solid walls around us and a roof over us, along with the knowledge that our doors are double locked and dead bolted. A healthy balance in the bank gives us confidence that our needs will be taken care of. We like insurance that covers us in case of catastrophe and pension plans that promise to sustain us in our old age. Having our family safe and well and near at hand is reassuring.

Perhaps you've noticed that many businesses create their

names and do their advertising in such a way as to capitalize on our need for security. Banks, storage companies, title companies, insurance companies, etc., use the word "security" in their names. Their purpose in using the word, of course, is to "hook" us at the depth of this great need and thus persuade us to acquire their products because we have been persuaded that doing so will make us feel safe.

As Christians, of course, we already possess the greatest and the only real security that exists. To borrow a phrase from a well-known insurance company, we have a "piece of the Rock." Actually we have more than a piece. The Rock of Ages is our firm foundation. A great paradox of the gospel is that God calls us to place our faith and trust in this rock, which we can neither see with our eyes nor feel with our hands. The rock that we cannot purchase with money or find in any quarry. This kind of trust is tough for us humans to feel because it seems alien to our daily experience.

Ever since the children of Israel melted down their jewelry to make a golden calf to worship (Moses having been delayed in coming down the mountain as he talked to this God whom they could neither see nor touch), people have been placing more faith in material security than in the God who created the world out of nothing and installed us here as its caretakers. No matter how solid our security arrangements may seem, however, they can never provide genuine security. In our hearts we know this because we have seen disaster strike in an instant—a fire, a flood, an earthquake, a dread disease, a divorce or the threat of a divorce, a stock market crash, a tragic accident. But when we build our lives on the Rock of Ages, our Lord Jesus Christ, our security is absolute.

The writer of Hebrews quotes God as saying, "Yet once more I will shake not only the earth but also the heaven" (12:26). The word "shake" is the same word used in Luke's version of the two builders when he says that the flood could not shake the house with the firm foundation. The writer explains, "This phrase, 'Yet once more,' indicates the removal of what is shaken—that is, created things—so that what cannot be shaken may remain. Therefore, since we are receiving a kingdom that cannot be shaken, let us give thanks, by which we offer to God an acceptable worship with reverence and awe" (Hebrews 12:27-28). The writer of Hebrews also tells us that "faith is the assurance of things hoped for, the conviction of things not seen" (Hebrews 11:1). These are strong words, but they are weak compared to the original Greek words. The word translated "assurance," *hupostasis,* means something solid and foundational, something basic. This is not just positive thinking based on imagination or even logic. It's not a pat on the back that says "everything's going to turn out OK," when we're pretty sure it's not. It's rock solid—a concrete reality as real and as firm as the foundation under your house. (Or in the case of the foolish builder, much firmer than the foundation under his house.) Faith is the assurance of things hoped for, the conviction of things not seen. This word "conviction" is a translation of two Greek words. One of them repeats the idea of a concrete reality that is foundational and of great importance. The other word suggests a thought or belief that has been tested or cross-examined. It's the kind of product that has been subjected to numerous road tests and stress tests that have earned it a certificate of quality. So when the writer says that faith is the conviction or the evidence of things not seen, it means that this faith is based on something that has been tested and has been found to be authentic.

What is it that meets this test? What is it that the author can say is rock solid, foundational, and thoroughly tested for authenticity? It's what God has done. The power of God working from the creation of the world through the lives of the great saints to Jesus' work on the cross to God's very working in our own lives, which we have seen with our own eyes. This is what God has done for us. This is the very basis and the very foundation of our faith. It is what reminds us that ultimately everything is OK. Life *is* secure.

While we are in fact safe on the ultimate level, we do not always feel safe. Dietrich Bonhoeffer describes the paradox: "The disciple is dragged out of his relative security into a life of absolute insecurity (that is, in truth, into the absolute security and safety of the fellowship of Jesus)."[1] Matthew left behind the lucrative (and somewhat shady) business of collecting taxes. James and John left behind the security of the family business. A number of named and unnamed women gave substantial sums from their life savings to support Jesus and his wandering band. All of them gave up the privilege of having a settled and stable home life in order to follow Jesus. The great saints listed in Hebrews 11 have similar tales to tell—from Noah to Rahab to Barak. What separates these people from their contemporaries is their willingness to risk a certain amount of material insecurity in this present life in order to pursue the promise of God, which they believed to be quite trustworthy.

Psalm 46 echoes the same trust that the city of God "shall not be moved" (46:5)—read "is unshakable." The reason? "God is in the midst of the city" (Psalm 46:5). The unshakableness of the city of God is not based on its fortifications, its military tactics, its intelligence, or any other kind of material strength. No! "God is in the midst." Similarly, we do not find our security in what we have or even in how we feel. We find it in a relationship—a relationship with our God. When God is in our midst, we enjoy real, everlasting security.

This security is real even when it is not apparent. In the Old Testament book of 2 Kings, there is a great story about the prophet Elisha, who was always managing to get himself into a tight spot. His prophetic gift enabled him to divine the military strategies of Israel's enemies, which he naturally passed on to the king of Israel. When the king of Aram (a state in the region that clashed with Israel) heard how Israel had managed to thwart his attacks, he sent an armored division to capture Elisha. During the night a huge battalion surrounded the city. In the morning Elisha's servant was terrified to see the enemy army with all its horses and chariots. "Alas, master! What shall we do?" the servant cried. Elisha was unruffled. "Do not be afraid, for there are more with us than there are with them." I can imagine the servant looking this way and that but seeing just himself and Elisha. And a passel of enemies. Then Elisha prays, "O LORD, please open his eyes that he may see" (2 Kings 6:15-17). Suddenly the servant sees the army of the Lord—horses and chariots of fire—surrounding Elisha. It takes the eyes of faith to see the unseen, yet the security that God provides when we place our life in God's hands is very real.

The real issue here is how to hold lightly whatever material security we have achieved—bearing in mind that it is flimsy at best—while clinging with all our might to God and God's kingdom. This begins to get a bit personal, I know. Perhaps it's time to acknowledge my own struggle with this. The first time I was conscious of this tension within me was when I had to move in order to respond to God's call to me. I had to leave what was both secure and comfortable to me in the upper Midwest—my family and friends and familiar territory—to go to southern California, where an unknown future awaited me at seminary. I remember that during orientation week someone congratulated me on being brave enough to undertake such a move all alone. But I wasn't brave. After that conversation, I went back to my room and cried my eyes out because I was scared to death of what I was doing. Still, I knew that God was calling me, and I knew that in order to follow, I had to take the risk. That was not the end of it (even though I thought it might be), since human beings collect security as a sunken ship collects barnacles. Time and time again, God has called me out of a place that has become comfortable and familiar and has called me into what seems to be insecurity. It hasn't always meant moving geographically. Some of the riskiest journeys have been emotional ones.

Our Response to God's Grace

This leads us to an important point: we are not the initiators when it comes to our relationship with God—God is. The rhythm of grace is that God acts, and the people of God respond. This is always the way it is in our relationship with God: God initiates, we respond. Even in our prayers of petition, asking God for things, there is an element of knowing that God has already shown faithfulness . . . that we would not even be there on our knees if we were not in some measure aware of God's grace.

Let me share a couple of familiar examples. One is the Ten Commandments, which are often understood simply as arbitrary rules that God has set down for us to obey. But they are more than just rules, and they are far from arbitrary. They are rules that show how people are to live in response to what God has done. Consider what went on between God and God's people before the Ten Commandments were given. They had been slaves in Egypt, but God had liberated them by leading them out, employing impressive miracles and the leadership of Moses. God then started them off toward the Promised Land. Listen to the way the Ten Commandments begin: "I am the LORD your God, who brought you up out of the land of Egypt, . . . [therefore] you shall have no other gods before me" (Exodus 20:2-3). The "therefore" is implied. God was not demanding obedience out of the blue. God had already acted. God had built the foundation of their relationship. God had already saved them, so the list of commands was far from arbitrary. Obedience was a way to express their gratitude for what God had done, a way of keeping up their end of the relationship.

We see another example of this in the structure of the New Testament book of Romans. The apostle Paul has arranged his material in such a way that he spends the first eleven chapters writing about what God has done for us in Jesus Christ. He ends chapter 11 with a lyrical statement of praise. Then he begins chapter 12: "I appeal to you therefore, brothers and sisters, by the mercies of God, to present your bodies as a living sacrifice" (Romans 12:1), going on to talk about the Christian's call to ministry and the spiritual gifts. Here again we see the clear pattern of God's initiation and our response. Earlier in Romans, Paul writes that "while we still were sinners Christ died for us" (Romans 5:8). God has given; we respond by giving ourselves to God in ministry.

God has given, we respond. It is a rhythm that has continued between God and the people of God for generations. It is such a strong theme in Scripture that I have come to believe that God never calls us *to* anything without first giving. Without first saving. This is what provides the firm footing for each turning point. We can step into the future with confidence because of what God has done.

A Greek word has made its way into our English language that shows this truth in a most profound way. The word is *eucharisteo,* and it means "to give thanks" or "to praise." The English word—Eucharist—is a synonym for the Lord's Supper, or Holy Communion.

At the heart of the word *eucharisteo* is the root *charis,* which can mean anything that makes someone rejoice or makes someone happy. It also means "grace." God's grace. Adding the prefix *eu*-magnifies the meaning. Together with the verb ending, the word means "to give thanks." It becomes clear, then, that the biblical notion of thanksgiving has at its heart the grace of God.

It was customary in first-century Jewish homes for the head of the house to take, at the beginning of a meal, a piece of bread and recite the thanksgiving (we call it saying "grace"), which went something like this: "Blessed art thou, O Lord, our God, King of the universe, who bringest forth bread from the earth." And the others would say "amen." Then the head of the house would eat a fragment of the bread and share it with those gathered.

This ought to sound awfully familiar, since we know that "the Lord Jesus on the night when he was betrayed took a loaf of bread, and when he had given thanks, he broke it and said, 'This is my body that is for you'" (1 Corinthians 11:23-24). In doing this, Jesus took an existing custom and infused it with new meaning. The prayer of "thanksgiving" (saying "grace"), which has as its heart the grace of God, grew into a remembrance of the grace of God that was expressed in the crucifixion of Jesus Christ.

When members of the early church celebrated the Lord's Supper, they included the "thanksgiving" as a part of the celebration. By the second century, the word *eucharistia* had already become a technical term that referred to the entire celebration. So it is that a word meaning "thank you" has come to mean the meal at which we remember what God has done for us in Jesus Christ. These days the term "Eucharist" tends to be used mostly by the more liturgical churches—the Roman Catholic and the Episcopalian, for example. For many years of my own ministry, I avoided using this term because it seemed to imply a very ritualistic—stiffly formal—approach to the sacrament. The word seemed too "high church" to be used by someone whose perspective of the Lord's Supper is more intimate, communal, and family oriented.

More recently, however, I have reconsidered my thoughts on this subject. I am now more inclined to suggest a rediscovery of the word, along with a return to the word's original meaning. To celebrate the Eucharist is to give thanks in the deepest and most meaningful sense. It is also to lift the sacrament out of the doleful, dark mood that often accompanies it—as if the only thing we could think about during Communion is the awfulness of Jesus' death and the awfulness of our sins that sent him to the cross. There are other things to remember and to celebrate, such as the love of God and the fact that we are God's children. The Eucharist can become the joyful anticipation of the heavenly banquet as well. It is good to remember that at the heart of this celebration is the grace of God in Jesus Christ, who died for us. For this, we are most grateful.

"If God is for us, who is against us?" asks Paul. "He who did not withhold his own Son, but gave him up for all of us, will he not with him also give us everything else?" (Romans 8:31b-32). God has given. What remains for us is to say thank you.

Say Thank You!

Saying thank you is a deeply ingrained response. It is one of the first things that our parents taught us (most of us learned to say thank you long before we learned to tie our shoes), and it is one response that they frequently reminded us about. And they taught us to say it even when we didn't particularly like what we were given. My Aunt Louise had a particular knack for gift giving when I was a kid. We never knew what to expect, and the anticipation was always exciting. One Christmas when mohair sweaters were "in," my sisters and I each got a beautiful sweater. We loved them. Writing our thank you notes to Aunt Louise was easy that year. The problem for me was that I wanted all my gifts (whether from Aunt Louise or someone else) to be at that same level of "coolness." When the gifts we received were more mundane or something we didn't really like, writing a thank you letter was not so easy. But whatever the gift, Mom insisted.

When we say thank you, it implies that someone has given us something or has done something for us. We thank someone for something that has already been done. Yes, there are a few times when "thank you" is an initiation rather than a response, like the sign some folks hang on the wall that says "Thank you for Not Smoking." Or when the airline attendant announces, "Flight 203 has been delayed two hours. Thank you for your patience." By and large, though, when we give thanks, we are responding, not initiating.

Sometimes Ed and I like to go out for breakfast on our day off. We thank the waitress for bringing the menus, for bringing coffee, for bringing more coffee, for bringing the breakfast, for more coffee, and we even thank her for bringing the check and for taking our money. As we go through the day, we thank grocery store clerks and bank tellers (again, for taking our money!). On a work day we thank our secretary for doing projects, we thank people for stopping by or phoning, for doing tasks in the church, and on and on. I'm sure that your days are similar. Try counting sometime! Maybe we say it so often that we don't even notice it. We don't think about why we do it except that it is a habit, something our mother wanted us to learn, like tying our shoes. There's a lot more to it, though. Thankfulness is foundational to our Christian life. That may be surprising to some, since we were taught to "say thank you" mostly as a way of showing that we have good manners. But for the Christian, it's not just good manners. It is a way of life. Thanksgiving is "the very mainspring of Christian living,"[2] a "basic and lasting" element of the Christian life.[3] The opposite of an evil life is a thankful one.[4]

There is a legend about a person who discovered a barn where Satan stored various kinds of seeds. There were more bags of seed labeled "discouragement" than any other kind of seed. These seeds were particularly hardy and could grow in just about any kind of environment. When pressed, though, Satan was forced to admit that the one place that the seeds of discouragement could not grow was in a grateful heart.

Do not think that I am encouraging you to convince yourself that you *feel* thankful when you don't. I am not encouraging you to hide your anger toward God when things do not go the way you want them to. Thankfulness is not an emotion; it's not something that comes and goes with the tide, though we often talk about it as if it were. ("Thank God, that's over!" we say, or "I'm so thankful that things worked out this way," when what we mean is "whew, I feel good about that.") If we understand thanksgiving as an emotion, then it will depend on the emotional ups and downs of life. Whether or not we are thankful will depend on things going well and on our having feelings of thankfulness. But if we build a lifestyle of thankfulness on the solid foundation of God's grace, then we will be able to live thankfully, even when the storms of life assail us. Our turning, like our whole life of faith, will become a thankful response to what God has done. It's our way of saying thank you to God.

Living Our Thanks

A colleague of mine, who used to spend time visiting churches in native villages in Alaska, told me about a conversation that he had once. A native friend told him that while his people had many words describing different kinds of snow, they had no word for "thank you." Amazed, my colleague asked him, "Then how do you express gratitude?" "You live thankfully," was the reply.

I have come to believe that at the heart of the life of faith is the ability to give thanks to God in every circumstance—every life-altering (*kairos*) moment. What that means, in practical terms, is turning: turning from all that is destructive (bitterness, blaming, etc.), turning from our constant need to control things by overorganizing them, turning from our dependence on guilt and other addictive emotions. When we are on firm footing (the grace of God), we can turn to God even in the tough times, knowing that in all things, God works for our good.

Interlude: A Spring of Joy

I was walking along the banks of the Metolius River, fly rod in hand, when above the usual sounds of the river I heard a higher-decibel roar. Around the next bend in the river, I discovered the source of the sound. Out of the side of a rocky hill, crystal-clear water was gushing into the river. While "gushing" is not a common word in my vocabulary, I found that less powerful words, such as "seeping" or "trickling" or even "pouring" simply were inadequate to describe the sight and sound. The effect was almost violent as the water foamed and boiled from the side of that hill into a deep pool in the river. Nestled in the heart of Oregon's high desert, the Metolius is one of those amazing rivers that springs full blown at its headwaters from a mighty underground spring. Along its path, several more springs like this one feed the rushing stream. Standing on the opposite bank, I could feel as much as hear the roar of the water.

I found many other natural wonders there too—wild roses and columbine, tall pines, an occasional startled deer. In quieter spots on the river, the skitter of a little brown ground squirrel could be heard. But the dominant presence was the river itself, with its incredible source of life. In some spots, the Metolius was a quiet, meandering stream; in others, a raging torrent racing over rocky rapids. It was always on the move, yet always close at hand. Every time I return to the river, I pause at that same spot and wonder, as I did on that first visit, how the water keeps pouring out. Even in times of drought, the spring lives on.

On one special visit to the Metolius, the constancy of the river and the marvel of the gushing spring took on a profound significance for me. Each time I walked upstream or down, I would stop and listen, absorbing the sights and the sounds. I needed the soothing feeling that the place provided because I was weary and wounded. My husband and I were engrossed in a difficult and painful ministry. We both exhibited the classic signs of burnout and exhaustion. As we walked and fished, the Metolius began its healing work, soothing our jangled nerves as we hiked up and down its banks. Gradually, I began to sense more than the presence of the river as I walked and listened. God was there, in wordless comfort.

That Sunday morning, sitting in a friendly and familiar sanctuary not far from the river, we sang, along with the congregation, words from a familiar hymn:

All the way, my Savior leads me;
What have I to ask beside?
Can I doubt his tender mercy,
Who through life has been my guide?
Heavenly peace, divinest comfort,
Here by grace with me to dwell!
For I know whate'er befall me,
Jesus doeth all things well.

. . . .

Tho my weary steps may falter,
And my soul athirst may be,
Gushing from the Rock before me,
Lo! a spring of joy I see.[5]

The words of the old hymn were not lost on me. As the marvelous unending supply of spring water is to the Metolius, God's grace is to the weary servant of God. Like the spring, it neither seeps nor trickles. It gushes. And the supply is endless. In times of pain we may need to strain our ears to hear the distant sound around a bend or two in our journey. But it will be there. Forever.

PART TWO
Getting Real

CHAPTER 3

Full Stop before Turn

"What is REAL?" asked the Rabbit one day, when they were lying side by side near the nursery fender, before Nana came to tidy the room. "Does it mean having things that buzz inside you and a stick-out handle?"

"Real isn't how you are made," said the Skin Horse. "It's a thing that happens to you. When a child loves you for a long, long time, not just to play with, but REALLY loves you, then you become Real."

"Does it hurt?" asked the Rabbit.

"Sometimes," said the Skin Horse, for he was always truthful. "When you are Real you don't mind being hurt."

"Does it happen all at once, like being wound up," he asked, "or bit by bit?"

"It doesn't happen all at once," said the Skin Horse. "You become. It takes a long time. That's why it doesn't often happen to people who break easily, or have sharp edges, or who have to be carefully kept. Generally, by the time you are Real, most of your hair has been loved off, and your eyes drop out and you get loose in the joints and very shabby. But you can't be ugly, except to people who don't understand."

"I suppose you are Real?" said the Rabbit. And then he wished he had not said it, for he thought the Skin Horse might be sensitive. But the Skin Horse only smiled.

> "The Boy's Uncle made me Real," he said. "That was
> a great many years ago; but once you are Real you can't
> become unreal again. It lasts for always."
>   The Rabbit sighed. He thought it would be a long time
> before this magic called Real happened to him. He longed
> to become real, to know what it felt like; and yet the idea
> of growing shabby and losing his eyes and whiskers was
> rather sad. He wished that he could become it without
> these uncomfortable things happening to him.[1]

A popular slang expression a few years ago was "get real!" It
was directed at someone who made an outlandish proposal or was
not facing facts. For me, though, "getting real" signals a turning
point, one of the most significant that any of us will experience.
Not only is it important as a turning point in itself but it can also
influence other turning points as well. If we can learn the art of
"getting real," the other turning points in life will be more possible
because we will be able to face them more directly. "Getting real"
means facing the facts of our lives and dealing with those facts—
whatever they are. It means understanding what we are responsible for, as well as what we are not responsible for. It means
accepting responsibility and allowing others to be responsible as
well. It means resolving tough issues, forgiving and being forgiven, grieving, repenting, and in many ways becoming "weathered" (but not worn out) through living life.

Life Is Difficult

A few years ago I was shocked by a book entitled *The Road
Less Traveled* by psychiatrist M. Scott Peck. When I read it, I was
flat on my back with a sinus infection. What Peck said in the very
first sentence hit me between the eyes. "Life is difficult."[2]

It's true, isn't it? Life *is* difficult. Hardly an original idea, but
one that always merits thought. One high school girl described
her life this way:

> I feel seriously stressed out most of the time. My guidance
> counselor says my tests show I'm smart, but I'm having

trouble getting B's and C's, let alone A's. I went for math extra help every day last week—I even skipped lacrosse practice—and I still only got a C on the test. I'll never get into a good college at this rate! Then the lacrosse coach threatened to suspend me for cutting practice. Wonderful! Then at home I found a note from my mom saying to fix dinner because she was working late . . . again. Then my baby-sitting job canceled, and I really needed the money. I was ready to scream. I'm only 16! If these are the best years of my life, would somebody please shoot me? So, yeah, I went to a party that night and got bombed.[3]

There's no age discrimination when it comes to the difficulties of life. I belong to the generation that teeters precariously between adolescence and the nursing home. It's the one that is known as the "me" generation and the "Pepsi" generation. A newer term for my generation is the "sandwich" generation, referring to those of us who are feeling the stress of caring for aging parents while still raising children at home. I belong to the baby boom generation that has known unprecedented opportunity, as well as unprecedented stress. Ulcers and cardiovascular problems are more common than ever. So is depression. According to Leith Anderson,

depression has increased tenfold in the last two decades as people struggle to cope with the disappointments of unmet expectations.

Not the least of these disappointments is the boomers' failure to meet their own expectations. They have found themselves in a highly competitive world with 77,000,000 others vying for the same jobs, houses, and money. Many peaked early in their careers and have nowhere else to go.[4]

When I visit with my mom and stepdad, I see that the "golden years" are no picnic either. In their fifteen years of marriage, between the two of them, they have been through a heart bypass and several heart episodes, a hip replacement, diverticulitis, bronchitis, flu, pneumonia, and prostate cancer. It seems that just when we get accustomed to one stage of life, life throws a new curve at us, one we haven't seen before. Life is difficult at every age.

But what Peck points out in his book, as he gets beyond that first sentence, is that the difficulties in life are not unusual but normal. That is a shock because we would like it to be otherwise. In fact, we think it *ought* to be otherwise. Life should be fun, fair, or at least manageable. But it isn't. It's hard. People don't always treat us right. Things don't turn out the way we think they should. There are germs and evil. And we have to face that.

When we read the Bible we find a similar bit of shocking news. Becoming a Christian doesn't exempt us from trouble or make us immune to germs or cancer cells. In some ways life gets more difficult. Now that our allegiance is to Jesus Christ and the kingdom of God, we are on a mission that the world does not understand and often resists. Life *is* difficult. It's painful.

Sometimes, instead of facing and resolving painful issues, we buffer ourselves with layers of defense mechanisms. For many, these defense mechanisms very literally saved their lives during traumatic times. They may have been developed in childhood as survival skills in a dysfunctional or abusive family. But when the defensive behaviors hang on beyond the trauma, into adulthood or back into ordinary life, we may find our senses dulled and our boundaries blurred. We lose touch with our pain, which is the goal we were aiming for, but in the process we also lose touch with ourselves. Our symptoms, if we have any, are secondary and detached from the original source. When we try to "fix" what is wrong, it is often a matter of trying to calm the surface waters instead of plumbing the depths to find the source and seek a cure. In order to live the kind of eucharistic life that God intends, we must peel back those layers of buffer material and face the pain.

Influences

It is well known that many influences have a part in making us who and what we are. There is the genetic factor. When I go to the doctor for my annual physical, she not only asks me how I have been feeling but also asks me to review my family's medical history. One grandmother was diabetic. My father died of cancer, but the doctor reassures me it wasn't the kind with a genetic link. I inherited my mother's sneeze, my father's bunion joints, my Aunt Josephine's figure. When relatives from either side of the family came to visit us (I was the youngest), they all said that I resembled their side of the family!

Psychologists have pointed out how much influence other people can have on our emotional health. Our neuroses can often be traced to whether we were abused or spoiled by our parents, what kind of potty-training methods they used, or where we stood in the birth order. Our race and gender and the social standing of our families have also played a part.

It is important to recognize the influence other people have had on our emotional development. Even more so, it is crucial that we examine our feelings, behaviors, and choices, lest the influences of the past hold us captive.

Acting and Reacting

My husband, who has become something of an anger expert (learning from his own struggle as well as from study and counseling), describes anger as a secondary emotion. It comes from fear, frustration, or hurt, which in turn are rooted in loss. Many men in our culture are taught that it's not OK to be afraid or to express hurt—that would not be "macho." Because of this, many men learn to move quickly from hurt or fear to a defensive reaction of anger. They move so quickly that they are not even aware of the chain reaction taking place inside. A familiar "button" is pushed. Fear is felt, but anger is expressed. Men who are able to look past the anger to deeper feelings are also able to begin to change patterns of destructive behavior that have plagued them and their families. Those who are not willing to dig deeper typically repeat self-destructive and abusive patterns of behavior.

What is true for anger is also true for many other defense mechanisms as well. As we begin our journey to "getting real," I suggest that we examine some of our automatic responses and learn to switch from "autopilot" to "manual control." To begin, we need a bit of review from science class: for every action there is a reaction. The knowledge of this principle has helped creative geniuses to come up with everything from steam locomotives to jet engines to automobiles to pogo sticks. This idea of action and reaction is such a familiar part of life that most of us don't ordinarily give it a second thought. But we make use of it every day. We expect this principle to be in operation when we flip on a light switch or step on the accelerator (or the brake!).

This principle of action and reaction is not limited to the physical world. It also applies to social interactions. For every action there is a reaction. If you smack someone in the nose, chances are you'll get smacked back. If someone has you over for dinner, chances are you will feel obligated to reciprocate. "What goes around comes around," we say. A good 75-cent word for it is "reciprocity." In social terms we call it obligation. In military terms it's retaliation. It's the stuff that wars are made of—and family feuds. It's also the stuff that many dinner parties are made of. Most of us think that we have to act according to a predetermined action-reaction script that has been preprogrammed for us.

The principle of action and reaction also applies to our personal relationships. Sometimes we seem to be connected to one another by a rubber band of emotions that alternately pulls us toward each other and pushes us away from each other. And then we find ourselves caught in a reactive web of obligation or retaliation. Families experience this a great deal, even two-adult, three-dog families like mine. All Ed has to do is go out on the patio and light the barbecue, and he has two out of three Labradors dropping tennis balls at his feet. True to the principle, he automatically kicks the balls.

Certain interactions *do* become habits, and this is really the point. We can get so caught up in the push and pull of reciprocity that we lose our ability to think creatively and consider new possibilities. It is as if we had put ourselves on "automatic pilot" and then forgot where the manual controls are. We just react according to the familiar script. For many of us, the scripts were handed out early in childhood, and we have forgotten that we actually decided to act in certain ways.

Beyond just being a habit, though, reciprocity often becomes a dangerous game of one-upmanship. Perhaps you saw the episode of the TV show *Cheers* where Frasier learned that Lilith was having an affair. When Frasier learned about the affair, he asked whether the guy was married. When Lilith said that he was single, Frasier was disappointed. "I thought maybe I could bag his wife and then we'd be even."

But that's the problem, isn't it? There's no such thing as "even." It's a never ending spiral. At its best, reciprocity is self-seeking; at its worst, it creates a downward spiral of despair. Eye for eye, tooth for tooth, hate for hate, Christmas gift for Christmas gift, dinner invitation for dinner invitation.

Like all habits, reciprocity simplifies life. I don't have to think about when to brush my teeth. It's a habit, and I just do it after meals and before bed. When Ed and I have a disagreement, I don't have to think much about that, either, because we have some established patterns of interaction. I don't have to think about what to feel when some unsuspecting person refers to me as "the pastor's wife." A familiar feeling snaps instantly to attention. But when it comes to getting real, simple isn't always the best. Sometimes it helps to step back, think about a response, and consider what we're feeling and why—to examine our feelings and behaviors in light of our past and the decisions we have made as well as the present situation. Then we can learn to make new decisions about how to act instead of simply reacting as if our behavior were someone else's responsibility.

A Wild Ride

Let's examine the principle of action and reaction a bit more closely. A very common reactive behavior pattern is one that we have come to label "codependence." What is codependence? A codependent person is one who has let another person's behavior affect him or her, and who is obsessed with controlling that person's behavior. "The other person might be a child, an adult, a lover, a spouse, a brother, a sister, a grandparent, a parent, a client, or a best friend. He or she could be an alcoholic, a drug addict, a mentally or physically ill person" or just someone who gets sad from time to time.[5]

I first became aware of my own tendencies toward codependency when Ed and I got married. Ed knew that I didn't like his smoking. It affected my allergies and caused me to worry about his health. Besides, in my family smoking was simply not done. So he told me that he would quit when we got married. In fact, he told me that he had quit. But he was addicted, and he couldn't quit. So he started sneaking around, smoking in the bathroom or smoking outside. Sometimes I would catch a glimpse of him with a cigarette dangling out of his mouth—but I would pretend I didn't see him because it wasn't OK for me to be honest with him about what I saw. Finally he admitted his smoking. With that out in the open, I decided to help him quit by encouraging him (OK, nagging). After he had switched from smoking cigarettes to smoking a pipe, he even asked me to help him by hiding his pipes (he found them) and then by throwing them away. Finally, his doctor prescribed nicotine gum, which in time helped him stop smoking. But it didn't cure my codependence. Every time Ed deals with an issue—anger, dieting, etc.—I am right there, armed to the teeth with suggestions and help. The only problem is that I am going crazy because my sense of well-being depends on what's happening with him.

"Why do you see the speck in your neighbor's eye, but do not notice the log that is in your own eye?" Jesus once asked (Luke 6:41). Good question. Why *are* we so outwardly focused that we concentrate on the needs, problems, and concerns of other people, but we do not see our own needs and problems? This is the nature of the disease of codependency. We become so outwardly focused that our emotions ride the wild waves of the other person's behavior, emotions, or physical well-being. We codependents are so fixed on controlling our environment that we cannot see what is going on within us. What makes us this way?

In their book *Love Is a Choice,* Robert Hemfelt, Frank Minirth, and Paul Meier list three sources of codependence: "unmet emotional needs, lost childhood, and the compulsion to fix the dysfunctional family."[6] Dysfunctional is one of those 75-cent words that may seem vague but actually has a fairly simple meaning: a family that is dysfunctional does not provide the emotional bonding and nurturing that is necessary for children to grow up whole and healthy. Families that are dysfunctional usually have one or more of the following characteristics: (1) there is an alcoholic or other addict in the family; (2) one of the parents is emotionally unavailable; (3) the family has repressive rules that do not allow for the natural development of the child's individuality.[7]

A church family can be just as dysfunctional as a biological family. In fact, many of us were taught to be codependents in church. Here are some of the rules that you may find in a dysfunctional family:

1. It's not okay to talk about problems.
2. Feelings should not be expressed openly.
3. Communication is best when it is indirect, with one person acting as messenger between two others (triangulation).
4. Unrealistic expectations—to be strong, good, right, perfect. Make us proud.
5. Don't be "selfish."
6. Do as I say, not as I do.
7. It's not okay to play or to be playful.
8. Don't rock the boat.
9. Don't talk about sex.[8]
10. Some families add another rule—don't talk about God.

Stated simply, codependence is a reactive behavior pattern. But the original reaction occurred so long ago that most of us have forgotten about it. Most codependent adults made choices to adapt to or survive in a dysfunctional family. Those choices became habits that produced a lifestyle of codependent behavior. Some decided to try to control their parents' erratic behavior. Others learned to deny feelings and thoughts in order to conform to the system. We learned to cover up problems. We learned to be nice on the outside, no matter what was going on inside. In other words, we learned to be dishonest and controlling. The result is that we have given away the very center of our being—"that core of self that can think, feel, decide, and act—and [have] hand[ed] that center over to someone else, either to another person, or to the family, or to some institution or system. The codependent acts by 'remote control,' taking cues not from inside, but from that other source."[9] In other words, we give up the right to have our own feelings, our own opinions, our own decisions. We can only feel OK if someone else tells us that we are OK. We can only be sure of our decisions and opinions if someone else gives approval. And because we have a void right in the middle of us, we are always searching for the perfect someone or something to fill that empty space—and to direct our lives. This is what drives many people into unhealthy relationships. Often codependents meet someone who feels just right—someone who matches the dysfunction that they grew up with. Women who were abused as children tend to choose abusive husbands (and vice versa) because the relationship feels familiar. They have not experienced a healthy relationship, so they often are not able to choose a partner with whom they could build a healthy marriage.

There is only one thing that belongs in the void that we created when we gave away our center. You may think I'm going to say that God belongs there, but I'm not. Someone once said that each of us has a God-shaped vacuum in us that only God can fill, and that is very true. Only God can fill the "God spot" in our lives. But this is not the spot that I'm talking about. I'm talking about the core of being, the part of me that is truly, uniquely me, which has ideas, feelings, thoughts, and creativity. God does not want to displace my self or your self. God created each of us as unique individuals—uniquely different from God and from each other. And that is the way God wants it.

"Why do you notice the speck in your neighbor's eye and do not see the log that is in your own eye?" The answer is simple: because I have learned not to think, not to feel, not to experience my own inner pain. I have learned to ignore my own problems and to fix other people. "You hypocrite," Jesus says (Luke 6:42). Now that's not a nice thing to say! Shouldn't Jesus be nice? We codependents know that being nice is more important than any-thing else. It's more important to be nice than it is to be truthful. But Jesus thinks the opposite—it's better (healthier) to be honest than to be nice all the time and cover up problems. The word "hypocrite" comes from the ancient Greek stage and means "actor." The actors in the Greek plays would put on masks and then play their roles. That's what codependents do. We put on masks—niceness, togetherness, perfectness—that cover over our own issues and problems and pain and sin, and then we go about fixing the problems of the world. But we are trying to fix the unfixable when we try to change other people. There is only one person we can change—the one in the mirror. The ironic result of our efforts is that while we are busy trying to control other people, we are letting their behavior control us! And that is one wild ride.

During the summer before I started college, my father died and my mother decided to move from the farm to a house in town. After one week in college, I went home for the weekend to help her move. My uncle Eugene brought out one of his big, open grain trucks, and we loaded most of the furniture into it. The furniture was piled above the sides of the truck, so my uncle tied the furniture down as well as he could. On top of the heap was a chair from our living room. Eugene asked me to ride up there and "hold it down." (I weighed 105 pounds and I was going to hold it down!) So I climbed up and he took off. The sun had gone down and it was dark. As soon as the truck began to move, so did my chair. It swayed and rocked back and forth from the force of the wind. And so did I. The chair was tied down, but I wasn't. I tried to yell for him to stop, but my voice was lost in the night. For ten miles rocking and swaying, I prayed. I clung as hard as I could to that chair, but I was absolutely positive that my life was over. When we got to town and stopped in front of the house, my uncle asked me how the ride was. I said it was OK.

Codependency is a wild ride through life, with someone else behind the wheel. Our well-being is entirely in the hands of this other person. We may want to get off, but we are sure we can't. The good news is that we're wrong. We can get off. Before we can do that, we need to face reality, though, and the reality is that we have a problem. Jesus said, "first take the log out of your eye, and then you will see clearly" (Luke 6:42). In other words, the only way to get off the wild ride of codependency is, first, to learn to take responsibility for our own actions and decisions, and, second, to stop controlling other people.

A Very Heavy Feeling

Another reactive syndrome that tends to keep us from facing reality is something called shame. All of us have felt shame on one occasion or another. It's a familiar feeling, "a very heavy feeling. It is a feeling that we do not measure up and maybe never will measure up to the sorts of persons we are meant to be. The feeling, when we are conscious of it, gives us a vague disgust with ourselves, which in turn feels like a hunk of lead on our hearts."[10]

While the feeling is familiar, we may not be aware of the power we sometimes allow it to have in our lives. It's actually a *dis*-empowering influence that strikes without warning. We're feeling fine, going about our business—feeling good, capable, able to handle things—when all of a sudden, someone makes a snide remark, or we make a stupid mistake, or a thought crosses our mind. Then a dark feeling slithers its way up our spine and applies a stranglehold to our neck. Suddenly we're not feeling fine any more, not sure we can handle it, pretty sure that we'll never get it right. If there were a hole to crawl into, we'd do it.

We need to understand what shame is and where it comes from. Shame is not the same thing as guilt. We feel guilt when we do something that violates our own moral standards of right and wrong. Guilt, in that sense, is a good thing, since it tends to drive us toward confession, repentance, and change. We feel guilty for something that we do. But we feel shame for what we are. And when we feel shame, we are pretty sure that what we are is very bad and very deficient. Shame is paralyzing. In a relationship, family, or social group, shame is the opposite of love and respect. Instead of promoting the growth of the individuals within a family or social group, it tends to keep people down.

Like codependence, shame is usually "homegrown." The source of shame is systemic, which is to say that it's in the family system. We catch it from our interactions with other people in our families, in our schools, in our churches. How did shame get into the family system in the first place? Sometimes a distinct event or experience is at the heart of a particular family's shame. A family member committed a criminal act. Or a family member is a substance abuser. Or one of the parents abuses the kids. Or a child is born with a crippling defect. The event comes to define the family, which becomes wrapped in a cocoon of shame. In some families the precipitating event happened generations ago and became a family secret—so secret that no one remembers it. But they still experience the shame and transmit it to others.

The first time I experienced shame, I was knee-high to a fence post. In fact I was playing the role of a fence post at the time. One of my earliest memories is of a time when my mom and dad were planning to put a new fence around our yard. I was following them as they paced off the fence line and counted how many fence posts they would need. One of the overwhelming memories that I have of this moment is that I didn't even know my way around the yard yet. But I wanted to help. And I told them so. They were preoccupied, so they said, "OK why don't you stand here and be a fence post?" It sounded like an important job. So I did that. I stood very still as they walked around the corner of the lilac bushes and out of sight. When I couldn't see them anymore, I started to panic. When they didn't come back right away, panic turned to terror. Would they ever come back for me? I felt abandoned. I wanted to go find them, but I was sure I would get lost. Besides, I was told to be a fence post, so I stood there and waited! An eternity passed. When they finally did come back, they were amazed that I was still standing there. Where else would I be? They were amazed that I was frightened and that I was crying. They laughed. They told me I shouldn't be afraid. Later they described my behavior to my siblings, and they laughed too.

I felt ashamed. Obviously, I wasn't any good at being a fence post, and more to the point, I wasn't any good at being a little kid. I shouldn't have taken them literally—I should have known not to. I should have known my way around the yard. And I shouldn't have felt afraid. I know now that my parents meant me no harm. They didn't know what a significant event that was in my little life. But that's the way the seeds of shame sometimes get planted. A child has a hurtful experience. But no one validates the child's feelings, and the child comes to believe that he or she deserves to be hurt. How much more devastating this is when the hurtful experience is abuse. It sets up an emotional pattern that seems irreversible.

Many of us, perhaps most of us, received shaming messages as we grew up. But shame is like having a bag of popcorn in a roomful of people. You just can't keep it to yourself; you have to pass it around. So entire families, churches, and other social groupings can become caught up in this thing called shame. Some of us, as we grew up, learned to hide the shame whose wicked tendrils have run rampant and threaten to strangle our souls—by being the best at something, by trying to be perfect at everything, by working ourselves to death, or by being clowns and pretending that it doesn't matter—but it emerges from time to time, in barbed humor, in angry interchanges, in how we treat other people.

The most overwhelming impact of shame is a sense of worth-lessness—we believe that we are no good. And this is the crux of the issue. This is where our experience intersects with our belief system. What makes shame so difficult to fight is not just that we believe we're no good. Many of us believe that God believes it too. After all, the Bible does talk about issues like sin. And some theologians (notably John Calvin) call us "totally depraved," which sounds pretty bad. The church talks about the fact that Jesus came to die for our sins. And again, the emphasis is often on our failure. Our badness.

If we are going to get real, we need to understand how God really sees us. A couple of Bible passages will help point us in the right direction. The writer of Genesis tells of God's creative work in the beginning. After each day of creation, God surveys the day's work and says, "It's good." Then on the last day, when God made the man and the woman in God's image, God says, "It's very good." Very good. Like Adam and Eve, we are made in the image of God, and that's good. God created us good, not bad.

Yes, we do things that are wrong, sometimes very wrong, and we have to deal with that (the purpose of guilt is to lead us to change—*metanoia,* turning), but we were created good, in God's image. In John 3:16, a favorite verse of many Christians, we find the real reason why Jesus came to die for us. "For God so loved the world . . ." it says. God didn't send Jesus because we are rotten sinners. God sent Jesus because God loves us.

This is a major turning point for those of us who are stuck in shame. But we need to understand the part that we play in this. We have a choice to make, which will radically influence our life from this moment on: which message will we believe? Will we believe the message that we have been given since childhood— that we are no good? Or will we believe the message—from Scripture—that God made us in the image of God and that God loves us? The message we choose to believe will set the pattern for our lives. When shame is the driving force, life becomes powerless and joyless; shame predisposes us to failure. When we know that God loves us and even respects us, we can become all that we were meant to be.

The Past

A favorite movie of mine was *Forrest Gump*. One of Forrest Gump's gems of wisdom that I latched onto was this: it's interesting how some things are easier to remember than others. Math wasn't that easy for Forrest. But he remembered his first ride on the school bus. It's easy to see why. Most of the kids treated him with scorn and wouldn't give him a seat. But one little girl, Jenny, invited him to sit next to her. Jenny became his best friend and the recipient of his undying love.

Some of our experiences leave that kind of lasting impact. Many happen early in life. Someone in school calls us a nerd, and the name sticks. Or an adult whom we trusted betrays that trust by abusing us physically or emotionally. Or someone close to us dies. Or we are seduced into doing something that we know is wrong, and we end up hurting someone.

We have all had experiences that fall into this category. The event itself is in the past, but the pain is carried forward into the present. What do we do with this pain? We are feeling it now, but it is based on something that happened a long time ago. Many people advise us to leave the past behind and live for the present. "Get on with your life." "Let it go." "Rise above it." "Let bygones be bygones." Sometimes we can do that. We can just take a deep breath and say, OK, that's over with! But it's not always that simple, is it? The pain caused by some experiences lingers on stubbornly. Like the proverbial "bad penny," the feelings return ad nauseam. Still we persistently try to leave them behind because we think that's what we ought to do.

Ironically, just when we leave the past behind—without resolving the pain we experienced—the past can hold us captive. Henry Cloud and John Townsend tell the story of a young mother who went to a counselor because she was verbally abusing her young daughter. She wanted to stop, but felt that the behavior was uncontrollable.

"What have you tried so far?"
"Mostly memorizing Scripture about anger and taking

'timeouts' when I'm angry. But most of the time I can't
do that. By the time I know I'm angry, it's all over.
  "This may sound like a crazy question, Jill, but did you
ever experience anything like that when you were a
child?"
  "Well, I . . ." Unable to finish her sentence, she began
sobbing uncontrollably. It was a while before she was
able to talk again. When she did, she told horror stories
about how her mother screamed at her, about how verbally abusive her home had been. . . . She was reluctant
to speak about her traumatic past, Jill said, because of
what her pastor had taught her about looking at the past.
"The Bible says that old things are passed away and all
things are new," Jill told me. "I'm a new creation. How
can things from the past have any hold on me? I must
forget what lies behind and press on. I just need to depend
on the Holy Spirit to empower me, and I need to repent
of my anger, and I'm sure I'll be OK."
  "Have you tried that?" I asked her.
  Her look told me she had and that it had not worked.[11]

Jill's solution sounded "spiritual" but it didn't work because
under the surface waters of the memorized Bible verses was
denial, pure and simple. If we want to move strongly into the
future, toward wholeness, toward becoming the people God is
calling us to be, then we need to honestly face past events that are
still unresolved in us. When we simply try to close the door on
the past, we actually make matters worse. If we simply try to close
the door to the past when the pain is still there, we create a sort of
demilitarized zone between our conscious awareness and the past
experience. It's an emotional buffer zone.
  Many people take an extra glass of wine to dull the pain; some
people may try a little cocaine to keep their enthusiasm up. Others
may dig into their work really hard so that they can forget the pain.
Others have the mental capacity to just lock it away from conscious awareness. In each case the result is emotional numbness.
This lack of feeling is what many of us seek because it is more

tolerable than pain. What we need to realize is that pain has a purpose—it's a signal that something's wrong—and working through the pain is what leads to health and wholeness.

If we have lost someone or something important, we need to grieve. If someone has hurt us, we need to work through the feelings connected with that and gradually come to the point of being able to forgive. If we have injured someone else, we need to confess it and make amends. We need to face the pain and bring it into God's healing presence.

Victims No More

In recent years, the knowledge of how our present behavior is affected by past experiences, particularly traumatic or abusive ones, has played a big part in developing society's compassion for victims and has spurred programs to combat racism and other forms of oppression. Some who have committed reactionary crimes of passion after suffering years of abuse have found help instead of condemnation. Such social awareness has been a necessary part of the development of our modern consciousness. At the same time, some people get trapped in a kind of "victim mentality" and are unable (unwilling?) to break free from the past and to grow into a life of responsibility.

Some of us have been so aware of the effect that others have had on us that we no longer draw the line between ourselves and the other; what the other does (or did in the past) affects us so deeply that our emotional well-being depends on the other's behavior. We end up letting others make decisions for us or blaming others for decisions we really made ourselves. It's not that we "want" to—it's just that bondage, no matter how cruel, becomes familiar. For that reason bondage is sometimes chosen over freedom, which is unknown and therefore frightening. It's also because it's easier to remain a child (in terms of personal responsibility) than to become an adult.

I want to be very careful about the statement that I am about to make. Some people have been abused so severely that they are damaged for life. Their psyche or their physical being has been wounded to the point of no return. But most of us who have been victimized in one way or another, though scarred, have the potential for healing. And with healing comes responsibility for our own lives and our own decisions. We must move beyond blaming to accepting responsibility for our own lives.

For years I blamed my parents for the fact that I never learned to play the piano very well. I'm the youngest of four kids. My brother and my older sister took piano lessons from a teacher who lived in a town that was about seven miles from our farm. My parents drove them to town once a week for several years for their piano lessons. Both of them did very well, especially my brother, who now has a doctorate in piano and teaches in a university. When my other sister and I became old enough to take piano lessons, guess who we took lessons from? My brother. It seemed grossly unfair to me, and after a while I quit. And so it was my parents' fault that I never learned very much about the piano. That's what I thought for years, until I finally realized that my parents were not the only ones who had made a decision. I had also made a decision. I decided to quit.

Sometimes the influence of other people is so strong that the boundaries between us and them get blurry, and we don't always realize that we really do have a responsibility for ourselves and our own decisions. That's particularly true in families that do not value each other's feelings or respect each other's opinions. It's even more true in families where there is abuse, whether that abuse is verbal, physical, or sexual. Those who grow up being abused tend to lose sight of their boundaries and don't even realize that they have a right to control their own space—much less that they are responsible for themselves. Hubert Humphrey, following cancer surgery and a prognosis that gave him less than five years to live, was quoted as saying, "It isn't what they take from you that counts—it's what you do with what you have left."

And so we come to the notion of forgiveness. Forgiveness is a significant turning point that makes healing possible, despite the worst that has happened to us.

Forgiveness is a tough assignment, especially for those who have been sorely abused. According to Lewis Smedes, the notion of forgiveness seems "almost unnatural."[12] Indeed it does. Yet for those who want to get real, it is a necessary passage. When I think of how tough it is to forgive, I like to think about the image of the prophet at the end of the Old Testament book of Jonah. He is sitting at the edge of the city of Nineveh, hoping against hope that God will get some sense and destroy the wicked city. You may remember that God called Jonah to go and preach to Nineveh (capital city of the ancient Assyrian empire). Jonah refuses and boards a ship sailing toward Tarshish instead (far and away a more difficult and distant destination). A hurricane and three nights in the "Hotel Moby Dick" convince him that going to Nineveh is the better part of valor, so when God calls again, he goes. When he preaches to the Ninevites, they repent, which is surprising in itself. But what really galls Jonah is that God does not punish them. He concludes his mission to the city as a bitter, suicidal man. Why? Because Nineveh deserves to be destroyed. The Assyrians have sent army after army to destroy both Israel and Judah. Perhaps Jonah himself has not suffered physically, but his nation certainly has. And Jonah feels the pain of that.

Many wounded people experience what Jonah did. Their abusers do not receive the punishment they deserve, so the abused ones remain angry and bitter and unable to go on with life. They fail to realize that the real value of forgiveness is experienced by the one who does the forgiving, not the one being forgiven.

Corrie ten Boom, who was imprisoned in one of Hitler's worst concentration camps during World War II, makes this startling comment about forgiveness:

> Since the end of the war I had had a home in Holland for victims of Nazi brutality. Those who were able to forgive their former enemies were able also to return to the outside world and rebuild their lives, no matter what the

physical scars. Those who nursed their bitterness remained invalids. It was as simple and as horrible as that.[13]

We must understand, though, that forgiveness is not a cheap quantity. It should not be granted too quickly or too glibly. If it is, it may well be denial rather than forgiveness. Lewis Smedes describes the process of forgiveness in terms of four stages: hurt, hate, healing, and coming together (the last stage depends on the other person as well as yourself).[14] We do not jump to forgiveness, omitting the other stages. For the healing to be real, we must acknowledge the pain.

A part of being real is acknowledging that yes, we have been wronged. We do not deny the wrong that has been done. We do not deny the pain. But we do allow ourselves to heal and move on. This too is a part of getting real. No longer must we allow our wounds to define us.

Interlude: Return to the River

When we returned to the river this year, we found that it had changed. Halfway down the familiar trail, a giant Ponderosa pine that had been balanced precariously on the river's bank now lay prone in the water, its tangle of roots exposed to the trail. The tree was taller than the river was wide, and broken sections of the tree's top marched single file up the far side of the gorge. What a crack and splash that giant must have made when it toppled, taking a chunk of the trail with it. Farther down the trail, yet another tree and another had met their end in a similar way. Chunks of bark and small branches littered the shallow water by the bank. Other logs that had lain for years as permanent fixtures in certain places had moved downstream. "Must've been a tough winter," my husband commented. Indeed, it must have been, and the river bore the marks of nature's violence. I could relate. It had been a tough winter for us as well, and we brought our own battle scars with us. Our scars were not from the violence of nature, but they came from battles with life and work. This year we had become unemployed and were still smarting from a difficult departure. During this same visit to the river, a friend asked me when I had decided to frost my hair. I laughed. Like the fallen trees, my gray streaks were natural, products of the winter past.

The river and I are old friends by now, having spent time in seasons of joy and sorrow. Neither of us needed to hide the effects of a painful year. Its naked roots and my tears could be shared without embarrassment. In spite of changes, though, the river had lost none of its beauty. The spring still gushed. Wildflowers bloomed prolifically, and the river seemed fuller and swifter than ever. I noticed with new interest the trees that had fallen years ago, now relics of weathered beauty. It gave me hope that the aftermath of my own collisions with life need not result in ugliness or bitterness. Rather, the beauty of faith and hope can bloom—and I go on with strength.

"So we do not lose heart. Even though our outer nature is wasting away, our inner nature is being renewed day by day. For this slight momentary affliction is preparing us for an eternal weight of glory beyond all measure, because we look not at what can be seen but at what cannot be seen; for what can be seen is temporary, but what cannot be seen is eternal" (2 Corinthians 4:16-18).

CHAPTER 4

Truth and Freedom

Just as "getting real" includes resolving issues and feelings related to our past experiences, it also involves being honest about who we are and about our own actions. Jesus said that "the truth will make you free" (John 8:32), and most of us repeat the phrase "honesty is the best policy" easily enough. I suspect that most of us would say that we believe both statements. It sounds simple: just be truthful. But for most Americans on the brink of the twenty-first century, it's not simple at all. We have, in most instances, worked hard to buffer ourselves against reality because reality is just too painful. As we noted in chapter 3, we often find it preferable to insulate ourselves from hurts that have resulted from what other people have done rather than to address the hurts.

The Second Sin

When it comes to being truthful about our own behavior, most of us have followed in the footsteps of our foremother and forefather in sin, Adam and Eve. You know the story: a man, a woman, a garden, a command, a serpent, a piece of fruit. The first sin. But I submit that the first sin, trend setting as it was, was no more monumental in its effects than was the second—the cover-up (Edengate). The second sin added a dimension to the rebellion that intensified the first sin a hundredfold. Once they took a bite of the fruit, both sinners realized that what they had done was wrong.

If you were reading the story for the first time, you might expect that Adam and Eve, considering the intimacy of the garden and the warmth of their relationship with God, would run to God and confess quickly in order to restore the relationship. But no, they did what you or I would do—they went into denial. They sought to cover up what they had done. Of course the cover-up made the sin all the more obvious. And it began a never ending treadmill that their descendants have been stuck in ever since: sin—turn away—cover up—turn further—lie/deny. Confrontation with truth becomes the fork in the road—we either turn back to God (finding healing and renewal) or turn away to a life of deception (staying on the treadmill).

George Barna, a Christian futurist, describes America as a "self-deceived nation." "Our actions," he says, "are often empty efforts at becoming something that, deep inside, we know we are not." One area of self-deception that Barna describes is religion. Four out of five Americans claim to be "Christian," Barna says. But "that word has been made into a generic term referring to someone who is religious, believes in a universal force of some type or is simply a good person."[1]

Jesus once spoke to some religious folks, saying: "Now you Pharisees clean the outside of the cup and of the dish, but inside you are full of extortion and wickedness" (Luke 11:39). Paul warns that the time will come when people will be "holding to the outward form of godliness but denying its power" (2 Timothy 3:5). Many years earlier, in the days of the prophet Jeremiah, some false teachers were telling people, "Hey, everything's OK, don't worry about it." But everything wasn't OK. It was a lie. God's people were in desperate need of healing and forgiveness. Jeremiah accused those false prophets of having "treated the wound of my people carelessly, saying, 'peace, peace,' when there is no peace" (Jeremiah 6:14). Such comfort is like using a Band-Aid on a broken leg. It just doesn't do the trick.

When we read the Gospels, we see Jesus, time and time again, meeting people where they really are—not where they think they should be. The Pharisees think they should be holy and sinless, so they try to act as if they were. But Jesus confronts their sin, their lies. At Jacob's Well, Jesus meets a Samaritan woman whose life has been anything but sinless. He applauds her for telling the truth about her life, if not telling it in full. She is the first person to whom he reveals his identity as the Messiah. On the other hand, when Simon Peter brags about his courage, saying that he will go to the death with Jesus if need be, Jesus says, "No you won't, Peter; you'll deny me."

Jesus also meets *us* where we really are. Not where we think we should be—our Sunday "go to meetin'" behavior—but where we really are. In the same way that Jesus waited for the woman of Samaria at Jacob's Well, Jesus is waiting for us at the well of truth, and when we meet him there, he will lead us to where he wants us to be.

If we want to live whole, holy, joyful lives, we must get real. We must face the truth of our own behavior. This is far from easy:

> One recovering alcoholic related how he was oblivious to the effects of his drinking, in spite of what people said to him. Since he drank only beer, this man was certain he did not have an alcohol problem.
>
> Eventually this man became physically sick, and he could no longer deny that something was wrong. He concluded that by drinking half a case of beer daily, he was consuming too much *fluid.* So he switched to scotch and soda. When the physical symptoms got worse, he faulted the soda and switched to whiskey and water. As his symptoms got even worse, he eliminated *water.*[2]

It is not only alcoholics who have this difficulty facing the truth. In college I was involved in a Christian group where we learned to give what is called a "personal testimony." We were taught to tell the story of what we were like before we became Christians in contrast to what we were like after. It was like those "makeover" pictures you see in women's magazines. The "before" part of the story is really pretty ugly; the after part is all smiles and "isn't life great." This group of Christians included a young woman who had once been a prostitute, as well as a couple of people who had been substance abusers. These people had marvelous stories to tell about their Christian makeovers.

Some of the old hymns we used to sing told a similar story:

> I was once a sinner, but I came, pardon to receive from my Lord.
> This was freely given, and I found that He always kept his word.
> There's a new name written down in glory and it's mine, oh yes it's mine!
> And the white robed angels tell the story, "A sinner has come home."
> For there's a new name written down in glory, and it's mine, oh yes it's mine!
> With my sins forgiven I am bound for heaven, never more to roam.[3]

I loved listening to these dramatic testimonies and singing these songs. But I also felt somewhat uncomfortable because I had made my commitment to Christ when I was about six years old. I didn't have much of a conversion story to tell. The other source of my discomfort was that whatever sinning I had done took place on the Christian side of the makeover, which doesn't produce much of a testimony. It took me a long time to begin to understand that some of the beliefs I was living by had nothing to do with Christianity. They had everything to do with a belief system called perfectionism.

As Christians, we are called to strive for perfection, which means to become the best that we can be—all that God calls us to be in terms of Christian growth and maturity. We can do this because we understand that God has accepted us. This acceptance gives us a sense of self-worth, and it enables us to strive toward perfection in Christ.

But the perfectionist has quite a different motivation. For the perfectionist, anything less than perfection is failure. The source of this "need" for perfection is a poor self-image. The perfectionist is striving valiantly to achieve in order to find self-acceptance. This is also known as "overcompensation." When I was in high school, my goal was to graduate at the top of my class with a 4.0 average. (I achieved my goal but had to share the top spot with a friend.) If I didn't get 100 percent on a test, or at least the top grade in the class, I felt depressed. I had to make it to first chair in the band, and if I entered a contest, I had to win first place or I was not satisfied. Second was not acceptable, even though second was what I often achieved.

The myth of perfectionism for Christians is the idea that if I'm spiritual enough, if I try hard enough, I won't sin. Accepting this myth means that a great deal of tension is created when we do sin. It's like being caught in a trap. "What do you do when you uncover feelings in yourself that 'good Christians' aren't supposed to feel [lust, greed, hate, for instance]? Or when you find yourself doing things a 'good Christian' should not do?"[4]

The answer is pretty easy. Most of us begin with denial. Christians are supposed to be kind and loving and patient. Therefore, when we're feeling hateful, when we're thinking nasty thoughts about what we would like to do to so-and-so, we deny it because we know that we are not "supposed" to feel that way. In so doing, we begin to recreate reality around what we think we ought to be thinking and doing, rather than dealing with what we *are* thinking and doing. A sixth-century monk said that "the root of all disturbance, if one will go to its source, is that no one will blame himself."[6] Well, we perfectionists can't blame ourselves because that would admit imperfection!

It has been estimated that as much as 85 percent of all illness is psychosomatic, which is to say that emotional stress is the source. A great deal of the stress we Christians experience is a result of pretending to be what we are not—perfect. Imagine the devastation that some of my friends experienced, the ones in my college Christian group who had such great makeover stories to tell, when they slipped. When they sinned. For some the sense of failure was so great that they gave up the faith. You see, moral failure was not supposed to be a part of the victorious Christian life.

Perfectionism can be devastating for the church. According to Bruce Larson,

> What we need in the church are models who fail. Most of us fail more than we succeed. We find success once in a while, and we praise God. But much of what we do is a flop. Every parent and every spouse knows that. We all fail our cities, our world. We need to admit that. When we pretend that we once sinned but don't now, we produce a church where loneliness is rampant, a place where I know I'm not making it, but I assume everyone else is. The church is not a museum for finished products. It is a hospital for the sick.[5]

Not long ago, I read a newspaper article describing an upsurge in the popularity of "Christian" romance novels. The article listed a number of features that one publisher requires writers to include in these stories: the hero and heroine must not be divorced, the language must be clean (avoiding even such terms as "heck" and "darn"), there must be no explicit sexual language, etc. The list disturbed me because while the books (which sound a whole lot "better" than life) may encourage moral living, they are also very likely to give people the impression that Christians don't sin or fail. And that's hogwash. It would be much better to tell stories (as the Bible does) of people who fail conspicuously, learn that God still loves them, are redeemed by God, and find themselves changed and healed by God's forgiving love. And God uses them in spite of their sin and failure. That's real.

We are new creatures in Christ, and that opens up a whole new world of possibilities for transformation, for healing, for becoming the people we are meant to be. But oddly enough that transformation can only happen if we admit that we are still stumbling, bumbling sinners who need Jesus. Recognizing that some things that appear to be failure (notably the crucifixion) may prove to be the grace of God also puts a new spin on failure.

I still struggle with perfectionism. I still like to think that I can handle it, that I can rise above it. But I know I can't. Ed and I were having lunch with a colleague in the midst of a particularly stressful time in our ministry. The colleague was asking how he could pray for us. I decided to take a risk and said, "Well, you could pray for us, for our relationship. Sometimes all the stress sort of gets to us and we end up taking it out on each other." I don't know what I expected him to say in response, but what he did say surprised me. "If you weren't experiencing those kinds of problems, I'd be worried about you." In other words, that's normal. You're human.

Denial can also be a systemic issue. Whole groups of people can be in denial—such as families and churches. One person acts out (typically with addictive behavior or substance abuse), and others who know about it become accomplices by denying it and lying about it. The lies spin a web around the truth, which then becomes (almost) invisible to the casual observer. Those within the system are, for the most part, blind to it. I have known churches so accustomed to lying about such behavior that they no longer recognize the truth when they hear it or see it. Sometimes they actively fight against the truth's being revealed.

I have had the opportunity to be involved in a fair amount of conflict in my ministry, both as a contender and as an outside observer/consultant. Some of this conflict has been between individuals in a church or in a family. Other conflict has occurred between groups within a church; some has occurred between pastors and their churches, or between two churches, or even between a presbytery and a church. Conflict is common and is not necessarily to be avoided. Conflict shows us where our differences are, and it can be a significant growth experience if we allow it to be.

Over the years I have observed two ways of dealing with

conflict. One is conflict management, and the other is conflict resolution. If the chosen path is conflict management, the settlement discussion will stick pretty much to the "presenting problem" and seek to reach a compromise that allows the parties to move on. The problem with conflict management is that it seldom goes below the surface to discover root causes, nor does it tend to confront sin or address motive. Conflict resolution, on the other hand, is not afraid to get its hands dirty. This sort of process requires the parties to be honest, to confess failure if appropriate, to find the root causes of the conflict, and to find a way to resolve it, not just manage it.

I have found it interesting to observe too that it is not only negative truths that people hide from. When my husband is asked about his call to the ministry, he usually says, "For twenty-five years I ran as hard and as fast as I could away from my call." He did. In the process he ran through two marriages and several different jobs, trying to find something, anything, that he could be successful at and that would at the same time keep him out of the ministry. Instead, he ended up broke, alone, and suicidal. Only then was he willing to face the incredible truth: God was still calling him!

Jesus' Vision for Ministry

Something was lost and something was broken a long time ago when Adam and Eve took that first bite out of a piece of luscious, forbidden fruit. They lost their innocence and broke their relationship with God. That incident describes not only their lives but also ours. From Adam and Eve, our first parents, we have all inherited a taste for forbidden fruit—a tendency to sin. Each of us in our own way perpetuates humanity's separation from God. The entire history of humanity, from creation until now, is a history of brokenness: broken promises, broken relationships, broken hearts, broken lives. A loss of wholeness. In one way or another, we are all broken, and our goal of becoming whole again is always just out of reach. But the good news is that Jesus came into this broken world, he lived, he died, and he rose again so that we could recover our relationship with God and in that recovery find healing for all of our brokenness.

In Luke we find the first recorded sermon preached by Jesus (Luke 4:16-21). Using this passage, he presents what we today would call his "vision for ministry." He speaks of what he intends to do and what his purpose is.

> When he came to Nazareth, where he had been brought up, he went to the synagogue on the sabbath day, as was his custom. He stood up to read, and the scroll of the prophet Isaiah was given to him. He unrolled the scroll and found the place where it was written:
>
> > "The Spirit of the Lord is upon me,
> > because he has anointed me
> >   to bring good news to the poor.
> > He has sent me to proclaim release to the captives
> >   and recovery of sight to the blind,
> >   to let the oppressed go free,
> > to proclaim the year of the Lord's favor."
>
> And he rolled up the scroll, gave it back to the attendant, and sat down. The eyes of all in the synagogue were fixed on him. Then he began to say to them, "Today this scripture has been fulfilled in your hearing."

This is Jesus' vision for ministry. This is why he came: good news for the poor, release to the captives, recovery of sight for the blind, freedom for the oppressed. Jesus' ministry is about recovery. He knows that we are broken, and he wants us to get better. Beyond that, he has the power to make us better. There are several implications that I want to make sure you notice in this story. First, brokenness is a reality. People are oppressed, people are in bondage, people are blind and poor. If you think that something like bondage—slavery—is not a very contemporary idea, just ask any addict. An addict is a slave to a substance or a behavior. An addict is blind to his or her own need. And the first step to recovery is always a recognition of brokenness. Recovery begins when we acknowledge that we have become powerless over the substance or the process that has enslaved us. It has become our god. There is a whole lot of brokenness in the world that needs to be healed. It has been estimated that 96 percent of us are affected in some way by the addictive process. The people who came up with that percentage included the following categories in that 96 percent: "a person who is (1) in a love or marriage relationship with an alcoholic, (2) has one or more alcoholic parents or grandparents, or (3) grew up in an emotionally repressive family."[7] Clearly, addiction is a pervasive force in our homes, in the workplace, and in church. Brokenness is a reality.

Second, Christian recovery touches the very real wounds in our lives. Many people think of Christianity as being out of touch with the real world, as being about "spiritual" things that are vague and otherworldly and cannot be touched. But that is not biblical Christianity. When Jesus talks about blindness and oppression and poverty and bondage, he is saying that God wants to be involved in what is really going on in our lives. No matter what it is. When my niece Sara was about three (she's in college now), she learned at Sunday school that she could become a Christian by inviting Jesus into her heart. Sara was appalled. She said, "He won't want to go there. It's too dark in there!" But God is not afraid of the dark places in our hearts. And God does not avoid the tough areas of our lives. God wants to touch us where we really live. But sometimes we're embarrassed to let God go there. We feel safer keeping God at arm's length—at some sort of "spiritual" but unreal kind of level. So many times we feel that we have to show a perfect exterior to other people, especially at church. We are supposed to have it together. We don't want people to know we are broken. According to Pat Means, "Confession may be good for the soul, but it sure is bad for the reputation." If we want to recover, though, we have to get real about what's going on with us. Means continues, "Without being real, we'll never let God all the way in to do the kind of deep-down healing that's essential to true recovery."[8]

On this subject of getting real, I want to say a word about feelings. When we recover from a cold or the flu, we usually know that we are getting better when we start feeling better. But when we start to recover from any kind of addiction, we don't always feel better right away. Often, we feel worse. Bear in mind that the reason most of us became addicted in the first place was to escape some sort of pain. The addictive substance functioned as a numbing agent. As we begin to peel back the layers of addiction, what's underneath is the pain. We have to deal with the pain that we have been avoiding so long, however severe it may be. But that's OK because Jesus is not afraid of the realities of our lives. Besides, he has the power to heal us.

Third, after Jesus read the passage from Isaiah, he said, "Today this scripture has been fulfilled in your hearing." Many people think that Christianity is just about going to heaven some day in the future. Other people think it's just about something that happened a long time in the past. While each perspective includes part of the story, neither tells the whole story. The Bible tells us that God is involved in our lives today. Jesus' power to heal is not just a story from the past, and it's not just a promise for the future. Jesus has the power to touch us today, right where we are. Today Jesus will help us to take that first step or that fifty-first step in our recovery. It can start today if we take that first step today. Just remember that it is a journey that begins with the first small step of confession and lasts our whole life long. It's not magic, and it's not an instant fix—but the healing will come because Jesus has the power.

Recovery is not only a distant vision but also the "proof of the pudding." The reality of recovery proves that Jesus is who he says he is. When John the Baptist sat in prison, perhaps sensing his own imminent death, he sent messengers to Jesus, asking, "Are you the one who is to come, or are we to wait for another?" (Matthew 11:3). Jesus' answer is to the point: "Go and tell John what you hear and see: the blind receive their sight, the lame walk, the lepers are cleansed, the deaf hear, the dead are raised, and the poor have good news brought to them. And blessed is anyone who takes no offense at me" (vv. 4-6).

The proof of Jesus' identity, the validation of his ministry, was the reality of recovery. Jesus did not identify himself through fine points of theology or a fancy new program. He produced positive, constructive change in people's lives. This is the proof of the pudding for the contemporary church as well. If recovery is not taking place in our churches, then we have to ask, What are we? Are we followers of Jesus? Perhaps we need to be reminded of the healing power of the community of faith—power not of its own, but power that comes from knowing that when two or three or a thousand are gathered in his name, Jesus is in their midst. And Jesus has the power to heal and to restore.

Fencing In/Fencing Out

When we moved into our house in New Jersey, we installed a four-foot chain-link fence around the backyard. We needed to define the territory that belonged to our three Labradors. That fence lets the dogs know what their boundaries are—the extent of the territory that they can tear apart with their ball chasing antics. And they've taken ownership of that territory. Just let a rabbit, a groundhog, a cat, or some other vile creature venture in and the dogs let them know in no uncertain terms that their yard is off-limits.

Fences are familiar boundaries. So are the boundaries of a football field, the boundaries between towns and townships, states and nations. All of these boundaries mark what is inside our territory and what belongs to someone else's territory. We are responsible for what lies within our space, but not for what is in someone else's space.

When I was growing up, I shared a room with one of my sisters. She and I drew invisible lines all around the room, marking where our territories were. That was one way of marking out our personal space. Another kind of invisible boundary is called a personal boundary, or an emotional boundary. These boundaries define what we are uniquely responsible for and what we are not responsible for. For instance, acknowledging my own decision making in the piano lesson incident mentioned earlier was one of my first attempts at drawing healthy boundaries. Finally, I took responsibility for my own choice, and as a result I did a little healthy grieving. After all, maybe I could have become a decent pianist if I had stuck with it.

The boundaries in our relationships often become blurred or even erased, and we are not so clear about what we are responsible for and what we need to leave for someone else to handle. An important step in getting real lies in reestablishing these personal boundary lines. If our boundary lines have become blurred, or if we have never established personal boundaries, how do we go about developing a healthy sense of what is me and what is not me? What am I responsible for within my space, and what should I leave for you to take care of?

In their book *Boundaries,* Henry Cloud and John Townsend focus our attention on two phrases from the apostle Paul to illustrate the importance of good boundaries. The phrases come from Galatians 6:2-5. Paul encourages us to (1) "bear one another's burdens" (adding that this will "fulfill the law of Christ") and he says that (2) "all must carry their own loads." Confusing? Contradictory? Some definitions will help. A burden is something that goes well beyond what we would normally be expected to bear. You wouldn't expect one person, for instance, to carry an eight-hundred-pound weight across the street. A crisis or a disaster may create a burden that we simply cannot bear alone. People who lose their homes to a hurricane or tornado often need help from others to meet their physical needs and to get their lives back in order. To bear one another's burdens means to do for others what they cannot do for themselves. When we bear each other's burdens, we are fulfilling the law of Christ—we are living as he wants us to live.

When Paul says it is equally important to carry our own load, he is talking about our daily tasks. A load is like a briefcase or a purse that we use to carry around our daily responsibilities. These are the things that we are quite capable of carrying, and in fact we are uniquely responsible for carrying these things. In other words, these are things that no one can do for us. We are each uniquely responsible for our own feelings and opinions, for our choices and decisions, for doing our share of the work at home and on the job and in the church.

The difference between a burden and a load defines where the boundary is between me and you. Being clear about that definition helps us to know when "helping" is not helpful. "Problems arise when people act as if their 'boulders' are daily loads, and refuse help, or as if their 'daily loads' are boulders they shouldn't have to carry. The results of these two instances are either perpetual pain or irresponsibility."[9]

A classic example of this occurs in the alcoholic family, where the alcoholic withdraws from his or her responsibilities and into addiction. The codependent in the relationship attempts to rescue the addict from the consequences of his or her actions by calling the boss and making excuses or engaging in other kinds of cover-up activities. Healing begins when the codependent begins to draw some healthy boundaries and allows the alcoholic to face the consequences of the behavior. Sadly, things usually have to get worse before they can get better. And that's the problem for the codependent, who does not want to allow the addict to get hurt—in other words, to suffer the effects of his or her own actions.

For instance, a couple went to see a counselor about problems with their twenty-five-year-old son Bill.

> When I asked where Bill was, they answered, "Oh, he didn't want to come."
> "Why?" I asked.
> "Well, he doesn't think he has a problem," they replied.
> "Maybe he's right," I said, to their surprise.
> They recited a history of problems that had begun at a very young age. Bill had never been "quite up to snuff" in their eyes. In recent years he had exhibited problems

with drugs and an inability to stay in school and find a career.

It was apparent that they loved their son very much and were heartbroken over the way he was living. They had tried everything they knew to get him to change and live a responsible life, but all had failed. He was still using drugs, avoiding responsibility, and keeping questionable company.

They told me that they had always given him everything he needed. He had plenty of money at school so "he wouldn't have to work and he would have plenty of time for study and a social life." When he flunked out of one school, or stopped going to classes, they were more than happy to do everything they could to get him into another school, "where it might be better for him."

After they had talked for a while, I responded, "I think your son is right. He doesn't have a problem." You could have mistaken their expression for a snapshot; they stared at me in disbelief for a full minute. Finally the father said, "Did I hear you right? You don't think he has a problem?"

"That's correct," I said. "He doesn't have a problem. You do. He can do pretty much whatever he wants, no problem. You pay, you fret, you worry, you plan, you exert energy to keep him going. He doesn't have a problem because you have taken it from him. Those things should be his problem, but as it now stands, they are yours."[10]

The application of this principle is not limited to alcoholism, nor to family relationships. Ed and I were counseling a couple who were having marriage problems. We were bending over backward to spend time with them and work with them. We gave them exercises to do with each other at home and communication techniques to work on. Nothing seemed to work. Finally, they got mad at us because their relationship wasn't getting any better. We had a conversation with a psychologist about our frustration with this couple, and he said, "Any time you are working harder on someone's problem than they are, you've got a problem." The bells started to go off. If they weren't willing to work on their relationship, no amount of intervention on our part would fix it. It was time to stop rescuing them.

There are times when we are overburdened and need help from others. And that's appropriate. Grief and loss are two classic examples. But there is also within grief a load that only we can bear. Nobody can grieve for us. People can support us and be there for us, but they cannot do our grieving. We have to do that ourselves. When a pastor began to serve a particular church, she quickly learned that the part-time secretary had been hired just after her husband died. The predecessor had hired the woman because she needed something to take her mind off her grief, not because she was a good secretary (she wasn't). In other words, he tried to help her bear her load. And in the process, he short-circuited the grief process and saddled the church with an inept secretary.

This principle of boundaries relates to our relationship with God too. God is always on hand to help us with our burdens—things too heavy for us to carry alone. For instance, Jesus died for the forgiveness of our sins. This is something that we could not do for ourselves. Every day God does things for us that we cannot do for ourselves. But there are some things within that relationship that we must do. Nobody else can do them, and God won't do them for us. Only we ourselves can decide whether we are going to say yes or no to Christ's call to follow him. No one can do that for us. That's a part of our personal load.

When Ed and I began to organize a new church, we (with lots of help) made thirteen thousand phone calls in our local area to solicit interest in the new church. A particular phone call sticks in my mind. A man said to me, "My wife handles the religion in our family. I figure that when the time comes, God will let me in on the basis of what she's done." The man was not carrying his own load. It has been said that God doesn't have any grandchildren. It's true. God has children only. Each of us decides if we will accept the invitation to become a part of God's family. We can't ride into the Kingdom on someones else's shirttails.

Here again we can learn from the ones who started it all—Adam and Eve. When we take a close look at their experience in the garden of Eden, it can easily be seen as a problem with boundaries. First, of course, they crossed a boundary that they should not have crossed (the sin boundary). Then they covered it up. Their sudden need for clothing becomes highly symbolic for us. When we cross over the sin boundary, our first inclination is to cover up as well. We clothe the sin in layers of defense mechanisms, denial, and blaming. The overall result is the blurring of personal boundaries. We don't want to take responsibility for our actions. When God says to Adam, "Did you eat a piece of fruit?" Adam deflects the blame. "That woman—that woman *you* gave me—made me eat it. Not my fault." When God turns to Eve and asks, "Well, what have you done?" she responds similarly, "The devil made me do it. I was not responsible for my own actions." With those statements, Adam and Eve and all of humankind were well on their way to neuroses, ulcers, and high blood pressure, to say nothing of getting booted out of the garden of Eden.

Thanks for the Pain

I still remember my high school English teacher's favorite word: "THINK!" At least she used it a lot and said it loudly. That is the message I received from her and wish to pass on. Along with the message, "FEEL!" Learn who you are and where you have come from. Learn to know the difference between your space and someone else's. Discover the awesome freedom and responsibility of choice. When you do, you will be able to thank God for some things you probably never thanked God for before, like pain.

Ten people approached Jesus as he was walking along between Samaria and Galilee on his way to Jerusalem. They didn't come very close because they had the dreaded disease called leprosy

(Luke 17). Leprosy still exists today, but it is largely controllable. In the first century, though, the disease was incurable. As leprosy progresses, it creates disfigurement. Just as disastrous as the disfigurement is the numbness that is a typical side effect of the disease. People with leprosy are prone to injury and burns because they are no longer able to feel the warning signal called pain. After Jesus healed these ten lepers, one of them turned around to thank him. He was grateful to be healed, grateful once again to be able to feel pain.

While there's much more to be gleaned from this story, I want to stick with this one point: the man could feel pain once again, and he was grateful.

Pain is unpleasant, but it is a necessary part of life. It tells us that something is wrong (for instance, you have your hand on the burner). Pain also tells us that we need to do something (take your hand off the burner and put it in cold water). Pain, in this sense, exists for our good. To stop the pain, we need to go to the source. This is true in our emotional lives as well as our physical lives. Loss, for instance, creates great emotional pain. The only way to get rid of the pain is to face it—to allow ourselves to grieve. Most people go through a period of numbness as part of the experience of grief. This is quite normal. Then they move on through to pain and eventually to healing. For some, though, the numbness remains; they become "stuck" in their grief and never get to the pain. So they never quite experience healing either.

I was eighteen when my father died, old enough perhaps to have achieved some emotional maturity. Because I had grown in a family where feelings were not encouraged, especially "negative" feelings like emotional pain, I did not know what to do with the heavy load of grief that I was suddenly carrying. So I did what I always did. I buried my feelings and tried to pretend I was over it. Nearly twenty years later, I was vaguely aware that I had never quite finished with my grief. I had gotten stuck in the numb zone. The result was that I didn't feel the grief, but I was also not able to feel much of anything else, either. I had a recurrent dream during those years, in which my father was dying. I finally realized that my subconscious was trying to tell me something. I spent some time with a compassionate therapist who helped me to complete the grieving process. That summer, I made a pilgrimage from Alaska to South Dakota to place flowers on my father's grave and to shed a few tears. Following that experience, my dreams of my father changed. When he showed up in a dream (which happened less frequently), he was well. What I needed all those years, without realizing it, was something called recovery. The concept of recovery is big in secular America these days— recovery from a personal addiction or compulsion, from abuse or trauma, from grief or any other difficult issue. Christians often find it much more difficult to embrace recovery than people outside the faith. It's that perfectionistic tendency cropping up again: "I ought to be doing OK, so I'll pretend that I am."

Most Christians acknowledge their need for spiritual growth. A much smaller number of Christians acknowledge their need for recovery. What we need to understand is that for the Christian, spiritual growth and recovery go hand in hand. The Christian life is all about recovery, really. Our goal is to recover what was lost in the Fall, to heal what has been broken in our collisions with other people, and to restore God's image in imperfect human beings.

The ministry of recovery is one that churches must embrace. If we do not, we will not grow spiritually ourselves, nor will we have the ability to reach out to the real world we live in. The "magic" of the recovery process is based on a simple concept: honesty. Simple, yes, but easy? Not at all. "Recovery, like life, is difficult. It is difficult because it refuses to bury its head in the sand of deceit. It challenges well-constructed denial systems, it tests typical 'solutions,' and it requires change."[11]

Recovery is not easy, but it is the truth that sets us free. What is the truth that you need to face? Are you addicted? Codependent? Hurt? Abused? Have you lost your personal boundaries? If you have identified what your problem is, then I suggest finding an appropriate recovery group. There's no time like the present. Or you may prefer to find a compassionate counselor who has the appropriate skills to help you.

The whole world does not have to know about it, but you need to be honest with yourself and with God, and usually with an individual or group with whom you have a covenant of confidentiality. I know this is difficult. Most of us would rather just fix our own problems without having to tell someone else about the dark corners in our hearts. That is awkward and embarrassing. I know this because it's true for me. In facing the reality of my own issues, I did not want anyone to know what I was struggling with. In fact, I did not want anyone to know that I was struggling—period. But there have been times when I was not able to fix what was wrong on my own, even with prayer, whether the problem was sin or an old wound. At those times I needed the reflective and challenging presence of a trusted friend or counselor. There is something uniquely healing about verbalizing the truth. Having said it to one or more witnesses, we can often find that we can stop punishing ourselves and those around us. We can move on.

Interlude: The Last Zinnia

It was a crisp, cold autumn morning in central Oregon. Ed and I were interim copastors of the Presbyterian church in Redmond. Our experience there had been delightful. Not only did we enjoy our work but we also loved the environment. Less than an hour from the Metolius River, Redmond afforded us many happy fishing Mondays. And I had a wonderful garden. As I looked out the kitchen window that morning, even in the gray light of early morning, I could see that something was wrong. The squash leaves were dark and droopy. On the lawn there were white patches here and there. Jack Frost had paid his first nocturnal visit of the season. Since it was a Sunday, I didn't have time to go out and take a close look. When we got home from church, I went out to survey the damage. The beans were a total loss, and about half the tomatoes and squash vines were gone. But the squash themselves were fine. Overall, the damage was severe. But the zinnias got the worst of it. Where there had been a bright splash of red, yellow, and orange the day before was now an ugly, shriveled, mushy brown. Being the master of the obvious, I thought to myself, Should have picked them yesterday.

But I did have one zinnia that I had picked a day or two earlier. It was sitting in a vase in the kitchen window, with a row of tomatoes ripening at its feet. Three weeks later, the zinnia was still there, a bit bedraggled. It was hard to toss out that last zinnia because it had become more than just a flower in a vase. It was a symbol of the passing of summer. And it had been a great one, hard to give up.

But it was more than just summer or the passing of one season into another. It was a symbol of the fact that we would soon be leaving that ministry. It was an interim, and interims by their very nature are temporary. We knew it would be tough to leave that place, just as it was hard to give up the last zinnia sitting in the window.

Someone once said that God doesn't close one door without opening another. I think that the passing of seasons contains a hint of how God works with us in the seasons of our lives. Zinnias, sunflowers, and other garden flowers are called "annuals" because they go through their whole life cycle in one year. From seed to flower and back to seed, all in one summer. Perennials, like rhododendrons or lilacs, require the turning of many seasons to mature. The flowers in God's garden, the church, are more like the perennials. We don't mature all at once. We go through many seasons. The good news in the changing of seasons is that each time we say good-bye to one season and embrace the next, we take one more step toward being what God is calling us to be. We can't live all seasons at once. We have to take them one at a time. We have to let go of one in order to experience the next. Sometimes that's hard because we so enjoy the season we are in. We want to linger there. Things are pleasant, comfortable—and we don't always know what the next season will bring.

Then again, sometimes we *do* know, and we know it will be hard. The Preacher (the writer of Ecclesiastes) was right, though. There is a time for everything, and to every season we must turn.

PART THREE
Thanksliving

CHAPTER 5

Tough, Tougher, and Toughest

Picture this: The children of Israel are standing on the banks of the Red Sea after witnessing the most marvelous miracles anyone could imagine. They have lived in Egypt as slaves for generations, but Moses, by the power of God, has convinced Pharaoh to let them go. They are being led on this first leg of their journey to the Promised Land by a cloud during the day and by a pillar of fire at night. But Pharaoh has experienced a change of heart and now regrets his generosity. He and his chariots are now storming across the desert in hot pursuit of the Israelites. They overtake Moses and his followers as they are camped by the beach at the Red Sea. In front of the Israelites lies the sea. And they have no boats. Behind them in six hundred chariots are Pharaoh and his army. The Israelites are caught between the Egyptians and the deep blue sea.

What's Wrong with This Picture?

How would you have felt if you had been there, among the Israelites? Here's how they felt: "Is it because there were no graves in Egypt that you have taken us away to die in the wilderness?" they say to Moses (Exodus 14:11). In other words, "Hey, we told you we would rather stay in the first place. Now look, we are about to die!" Freeze the action at this point, with the

ex-slaves shaking their fists at their liberator. Pin this picture up
on the bulletin board of your mind and ask yourself, "What's
wrong with this picture?"

For the moment, let's shift our attention to another story, also
about a liberator and his followers and a body of water (Matthew
14). This time it is Jesus and his disciples on the Sea of Galilee.
Jesus has stayed on shore, while the disciples have gone out in a
boat. The Sea of Galilee is prone to sudden storms, and one of
those sudden storms hits when the disciples' boat is in the middle
of the lake. Try as they might, they cannot make any headway
against the contrary winds. It is the middle of the night when
someone spots a lone figure walking toward them on top of the
water. They are afraid, of course, but not for long. When the figure
cries out to them, "Hey guys, it's me, don't be afraid," they see
that it's Jesus. Peter, true to his impulsive nature, says, "Lord, if
it's really you, just say the word and I'll be out there walking with
you." So Jesus calls his bluff. "Come on!" Peter leaps out of the
boat, walks a few bold steps, and suddenly begins to sink. There
he is, flailing and yelling for help.

Here's where I want you to freeze the action in this story—at
the moment of Peter's helplessness. Pin up this picture of Peter
flailing about in the water beside the one of the Israelites.

Perhaps you have found yourself in similar situations. Times
when you felt trapped, vulnerable, defeated. Hemmed in by
insurmountable problems, uncooperative people, or unfavorable
circumstances. And there is no way out. Nowhere to go. No help
in sight. This is one aspect of familiar Bible stories that we tend
to ignore because we know the end of the story. We know that
God is going to open a pathway in the Red Sea, but the children
of Israel don't. We know that Jesus is going to reach down and
pull Peter up and then calm the storm. But Peter doesn't.

So, what is wrong with these pictures? Absolutely nothing. The
Israelites and Peter are right where God wants them. When we
understand this, we will begin to grasp an important truth about
our relationship with God. We do not know the end of our own

story, but we are called to trust God in the midst of deep despair or great trauma. It's not that God enjoys watching human anguish. God wants our trust; God wants us to experience the power of God. As long as we think that we can "handle" everything, we are not likely to see God's hand in the midst of our daily lives. But maneuver us into an impossible situation, and you'll see us squirm! At these times—these turning points—we are vulnerable and open to the possibility of miracles, of God working in our lives.

Between the Egyptians and the Deep Blue Sea

Perhaps you have heard, as I have, that in the Chinese language the word "crisis" is made up of two characters: one meaning "danger" and the other meaning "opportunity." The Chinese language captures the essence of the kind of turning point that I want you to consider in this chapter: the times when we are pressed to the wall and forced to decide, yet have no idea what to decide. We are forced to move ahead when the trail looks bleak at best and when it leads to the edge of a cliff at worst. When we are more than a little convinced that the light at the end of the tunnel is a freight train barreling our way. These are *kairos* moments in which our turning to God can have a special kind of grace.

"I am about to do a new thing," God says (Isaiah 43:19). Good! Newness is what we want, what we crave. The problem is that God has a habit of making this statement when things are at their absolute worst. When hope is but a fading dream.

I felt like an Israelite caught between the Egyptians and the deep blue sea when Ed and I were talking about leaving our ministry in Alaska. We had served there just two years; it had been a "best of times, worst of times" kind of experience. It had brought out both the best and the worst in us and in the congregation. Life in Alaska was dramatic from beginning to end. From moose in our front yard to glaciers within driving distance, to several feet of snow on our roof, to intense conflict in the congregation, the

Alaska experience was memorable. It was our first copastorate, which added interest to the learning curve. To say the least, it was draining. Add to that the chemical reaction that our bodies experienced with the dramatic changes in hours of light and dark, and after two years, we were asking ourselves the big question, To leave or not to leave? Ed was already convinced it was time to leave. I wasn't so sure. I don't like good-byes, even when the relationship has been less than perfect. Besides, we had bought our first house just a year earlier. The bottom had dropped out of the oil market and real estate prices followed the slide, making it feasible for us to buy a house for the first time in our marriage. But the market continued to find new bottoms, and people were leaving Alaska in droves. There were houses for sale on every block. It was not unusual for people to simply leave their house behind and suffer the consequences. Those who stuck it out and waited for a buyer had to pay the difference between market value and the balance of their loan (often a hefty sum). We went to our real estate agent, who had become a good friend. Virginia told us that (1) there was no way we were going to sell our house in the current market; and (2) if we somehow managed to find a buyer, there was no way we could get out of it what we owed. And that was the good news. We had no financial reserves. In spite of the real estate prognosis, we decided to set the asking price at the value of our mortgage, with the buyer paying all closing costs (which, of course, was unheard of in that market).

I regarded our action as a sort of a "fleece" that we were putting out, testing whether God was leading us to move on or whether it was just our own restlessness. We had some time, since we had not begun a search process for a new position. In the Presbyterian call system, that could easily take a year or longer. With little hope, we filled out the real estate paperwork and sent Virginia off on what we were sure was a wild goose chase. We asked God for guidance and grace. The next day, Virginia called and said that another agent had asked her about a house for a particular family. She immediately thought about our house. A day later they came to see the house, fell in love with it, and immediately agreed to our terms. Virginia had not even had time to put up a For Sale sign. Ironically, that put us in a different dilemma: we had to find a rental quickly where we could spend our last six months in Alaska.

Much more dramatic is the story of my friend Kim, whom we met while Ed and I were serving a church in Marysville, California. Kim had grown up in the community where the church was, and though she had some background in Christianity, she and her family were unchurched. As mentioned in chapter 1, it was a personal crisis—breast cancer—that created a desire in her to find God, and in the process, some answers. Kim's crisis began on December 28, 1990, with the discovery of the lump in her breast. Her initial response was that of most thirty-year-olds: "It's nothing." On the advice of Steve, her med-student brother, she went through the typical battery of medical tests. While the doctor was initially optimistic (saying he would "bet his life" it wasn't cancer), the news quickly went from bad to worse. The biopsy was positive. During the mastectomy, the doctors discovered that the cancer had spread to ten out of eighteen lymph nodes. One was as large as the original tumor. Later, the report from the oncologist indicated that with conventional chemotherapy, Kim had only a 15 percent chance of being alive in three to five years. Because of her age and the extent of the malignancy, the doctors recommended a bone-marrow transplant, a procedure still in the experimental stages for breast cancer. She was told that it could increase her chances of survival to 75 percent. It could also kill her. Three of the five patients who had already undergone the treatment at the hospital she was considering had died of what the doctors called "therapy-related complications." Their bodies could not tolerate the megadoses of chemotherapy.

The statistics had Kim pinned between the Egyptians and the deep blue sea. Her options left her angry, depressed, introspective. She looked for some reason why this was happening. Her main concern was not for herself, but for her three-and-a-half-year-old son. "That night," Kim said, "I cried out to God for forgiveness and begged him to allow me to raise my son. After that night many things in my life changed. I began to talk to God and to ask his guidance for my life. Still, I felt unsettled and anxious. I began a desperate search for reassurance. People kept telling me to just pray about it. I did, but things weren't getting any better." She finally reached her lowest point. "I was drowning in a deep well of despair, reaching up, but hope seemed as tough to grasp as a distant star. I was angry with God, and I remember praying in desperation, You know, God, if you can't tell me that I'm going to be OK and able to raise Bryan, then will you please tell someone else?"

That same day, Kim had a follow-up appointment with her surgeon. After the appointment, she stopped by the church to pray. Instead of staying in a pew as she usually did, she went up to the front of the sanctuary to the lectern where the big pulpit Bible was sitting open to Psalm 138. That seemed a bit strange to her, since that was not the passage that had been read on Sunday. Some of the verses leaped off the page at her. "Though I walk in the midst of trouble, you preserve me against the wrath of my enemies; you stretch out your hand, and your right hand delivers me. The LORD will fulfill his purpose for me; your steadfast love, O LORD endures forever." It felt like God was talking right to her. It certainly fit her situation. And it did make her feel a little better.

Less than five minutes after Kim got home, the phone rang. It was her Aunt Charlotte. "Hi, Kimmy, how are you doing?" she asked.

"I'm OK," Kim said. She said nothing about her experience at the church. Then Charlotte told Kim that she had just come from a prayer meeting with some women in her apartment building. One of the women had stopped everyone dead in their tracks by turning to Kim's aunt and saying, "Charlotte, I just want to tell you that your niece is going to be just fine."

"I know . . ." Charlotte had said, with a question mark in her voice.

"No!" the other woman insisted. "Just fine. She is going to be just fine!"

As soon as Aunt Charlotte told her that, Kim says she got goose bumps and sensed a sudden burst of energy. "I felt strong, and really happy for the first time in a long time."

From that moment on, Kim says she knew that she would get well. God had spoken to her in the sanctuary and again through her aunt. And Kim did get well. It was not the instantaneous and painless healing that I would have wished for her, though. It was a journey of healing that took her through conventional chemotherapy and then the risky bone marrow transplant. It was a healing that took months of her life.

Just before she went through the grueling bone-marrow transplant, Ed and I baptized Kim, her son, and her father in the same sanctuary where she had prayed. She insisted that the baptism take place before she go through the life and death risk, because she wanted to say thank you to God *before* the healing was complete.

In sharing this story, I don't mean to suggest that every desperate struggle can turn into a victory, if by victory we mean that everything turns out the way we want it to or the way we think it ought to. What I do mean to suggest is that our life with God is going somewhere. God has a plan, and our struggles can help us along in the right direction if we turn to God in the struggle. In fact, the outcome is not the point. Turning to God and finding grace is the point.

A good biblical example of this is Joseph, who was sold into slavery by his brothers. As the story progresses, we learn that God has a plan for Joseph that is not deterred by Joseph's enslavement. Joseph eventually rises to become second in power to Pharaoh in the land of Egypt, and that power leads to the salvation of his whole family, which is a turning point in the history of the whole nation of Israel. Many years after the precipitating event (the brothers' selling Joseph into slavery), when his brothers have joined him in Egypt, they fear what he will do in retaliation. But instead Joseph forgives them and says, "Even though you intended to do harm to me, God intended it for good" (Genesis 50:20). In the same way, God intends good in everything we experience, no matter what it is.

How can we make this truth work for us? In Romans 8, Paul says that the Holy Spirit "intercedes for us with sighs too deep for words" (v. 26). The Spirit prays through us and for us in ways we cannot pray for ourselves, at times when we know not what to pray. The Spirit thus provides the avenue for a turning point in the midst of our struggle. Later in the same chapter, Paul says that "all things work together for good for those who love God, who are called according to his purpose" (v. 28). Some translations say "in all things God works for good . . ." In either case, though the latter is more specific, the emphasis is on God, not on "all things." This shows that our relationship with God is not an amorphous sort of thing. God has a purpose for us. When we become Christians, the Holy Spirit comes to dwell in us, bringing along a new sense of destiny. Our lives are headed somewhere. There is purpose to life. We have a different perspective on our struggle. In his commentary on this passage, Karl Barth says that our love for God is "a desire so intense that it has already tasted its fulfillment, and therefore cannot be disturbed or extinguished."[1] When we have our hearts fixed on something of great importance, we are able to live through some very difficult experiences in order to get where we are headed.

Let's be clear about this destiny. Is it heaven, eternal life? That is certainly one way to describe it. But here Paul is talking about a different aspect of our destiny—something intensely personal. Following Paul's thought into verse 29 we read, "For those whom he foreknew he also predestined to be conformed to the image of his Son . . ." Try not to let the word "predestined" bother you too much. The word here is not referring to the idea that God chose to save some people and not to save others. The word means to set certain limits or goals ahead of time. Long before we were born, God decided that the goal for those of us who would become followers of Jesus was to be "conformed to the image of his son."

This is God's purpose for us, and it is to this end that the Holy Spirit sighs for us.

This puts a whole new spin on our prayers for ourselves, doesn't it? Think about it. When you're in trouble, or when you're sick, or suffering, or being mistreated, or just plain stressed out, what do you pray? Most people pray what I call a maintenance prayer—"Lord, please just help me make it through this day" or "this math exam" or "this trauma." Sometimes people pray "cosmetic" prayers. A good example is when someone who plans an outdoor wedding prays that it won't rain. When we're willing to be more creative, we ask God to help us reach the goals we have set for ourselves. Sometimes we even feel guilty about asking for God's help. Maybe we are asking for too much, we think, but the opposite is usually the truth. Most of the time we ask for far too little, and we settle for much less than what God wants to give. We often ask kids what they want to be when they grow up. Have you ever asked yourself what you want to be when you grow up—as a Christian? God wants to grow us up to be like Jesus. That's a tall order, one that we cannot fill on our own. It takes the prayers and the power of the Holy Spirit working in us, through good times and tough ones. An illustration that comes from George MacDonald (quoted by C. S. Lewis) is particularly helpful:

> Imagine yourself as a living house. God comes in to rebuild that house. At first, perhaps, you can understand what He is doing. He is getting the drains right and stopping the leaks in the roof and so on: you knew that those jobs needed doing and so you are not surprised. But presently he starts knocking the house about in a way that hurts abominably and does not seem to make sense. What on earth is He up to? The explanation is that He is building quite a different house from the one you thought of— throwing out a new wing here, putting on an extra floor there, running up towers, making courtyards. You thought you were going to be made into a decent little cottage: but He is building a palace. He intends to come and live in it Himself.[2]

Thanks for Nothing

I was no more than five years old when I lost my first best friend. That friend was a well loved and tattered stuffed toy rabbit. I don't remember what that rabbit looked like or how long I had it as much as I remember how I felt when I lost it. I was devastated. I looked everywhere for that silly rabbit: in my room, all over the house, even in the haymow, which was a favorite place to play. I asked everyone in my family to help me find the rabbit. They looked too, but nobody found it.

This may sound a bit crazy, but as I was growing up I really never stopped looking for it and never quite accepted the fact that it was lost forever. And I never found it. It was my first real loss. As such it is a memory deeply imprinted on my mind and heart. Most firmly imprinted are the feelings of frustration, helplessness, loneliness, and grief. These same familiar feelings have reemerged every time I have suffered a loss. They came back when I was eighteen and my father died. They returned when I was twenty-two and left behind everything that was familiar to me to go to seminary.

In the last several years the feelings have once again started gnawing at the edges of my heart from time to time because I am painfully aware of the aging of my parents' generation, as are most baby boomers. In the last few years I have lost an aunt, two uncles, a cousin, and a stepbrother. I have a big family, so there are more losses ahead.

I know that I am not alone in my experience with loss because loss is woven into the fabric of life from the day we are born until the day we die. It's not just about death, either. The experience of loss is much broader than that. We may lose a job or financial security, we may lose an opportunity, a game, our reputation, our car keys, a relationship, a dream, hope, or goal, our youth, our health, or our hair.

We cannot escape it. We would if we could because like pop quizzes and income tax, loss is stressful. It is painful. And it confronts us with a fact of life we would prefer to ignore: "that what hurts us cannot always be kissed and made better,"[3] that there are some things that we cannot control. No matter how many people and possessions we surround ourselves with, we face life alone. The popular author Judith Viorst tells of an eight-year-old who "was asked to provide a philosophical commentary on loss. A man of few words, he answered, 'Losing sucks.'"[4]

We may smooth over the language a bit, but I think most of us would agree that the boy hit the nail on the head. So what are we to do about this experience called loss—this experience that we do not welcome but cannot avoid? Most people's initial reaction to loss is denial. We try to pretend the loss is not real or is not permanent. Or that it doesn't matter. Another common reaction is to insulate ourselves against future loss. If you've lost a relationship, for example, you may decide to isolate yourself emotionally in order to avoid another loss. I have moved many times in my ministry. During certain times in my life, I have grown weary of saying good-bye to people whom I have grown close to and have shared deep and significant experiences with. At those times, I have turned inward to protect myself. People then perceived me as being cold and indifferent, when in reality I was suffering the pain of loss. I am convinced that loss can be an emotionally crippling experience if such defenses are allowed to hold sway for a long period of time. But I am equally convinced that, in the midst of loss, we can discover the grace of God and can experience a miraculous kind of recovery.

Jesus tells a couple of stories that lead us to this miracle, but they don't take us there right away. If we don't look closely, we may miss it. They are stories about a lost sheep and a lost coin.

> "Which one of you, having a hundred sheep and losing one of them, does not leave the ninety-nine in the wilderness and go after the one that is lost until he finds it? When he has found it, he lays it on his shoulders and rejoices. And when he comes home, he calls together his friends and neighbors, saying to them, 'Rejoice with me, for I have found my sheep that was lost.' Just so, I tell you,

there will be more joy in heaven over one sinner who repents than over ninety-nine righteous persons who need no repentance.

"Or what woman having ten silver coins, if she loses one of them, does not light a lamp, sweep the house, and search carefully until she finds it? When she has found it, she calls together her friends and neighbors, saying, 'Rejoice with me, for I have found the coin that I had lost.' Just so, I tell you, there is joy in the presence of the angels of God over one sinner who repents." (Luke 15:4-10)

Most of us, I suspect, relate very easily to the experience of the shepherd who leaves ninety-nine sheep to find the one that has strayed and the woman who goes into a frenzy of housecleaning to find the missing coin. Which of us has not gone into the same frantic action for a lost pet, a child, car keys, or even a bill that accidentally got thrown into the trash? And we can feel with the shepherd and the woman the relief of finding what was lost because we have had that experience too.

Once I went to the bank and drew out twenty dollars. On that same day I performed a wedding. I couldn't find the little folder that I usually use for such occasions, so I borrowed Ed's. The next day I was searching for my twenty-dollar bill, and it turned up missing. Since it was in one of those little bank envelopes, I thought perhaps it had gotten thrown away. I looked through the kitchen trash as well as the garbage cans more than once. I kept my eyes peeled for several days, hoping the money would be recovered. But it wasn't. About six months later, when Ed was getting ready for a funeral, he noticed a bank envelope in his wedding and funeral folder. Inside the envelope was my twenty dollars. Since it was February, I used the money to buy him a present for Valentine's Day!

If we read the parables only with this thought of loss and recovery, though, they give us little comfort. Who wouldn't feel better after recovering something that was lost? The real struggle, as well as the real questioning, begins when we lose something and don't get it back—when the loss is permanent. This is when we flail about, searching for peace, searching for meaning, wondering where God is.

Where *is* God in these stories? This question brings us closer to the real miracle of recovery. And for that matter, what role do we play in these stories? As the stories conclude, Jesus pulls a "prince and the pauper" switch on us. At the end of the lost sheep story he says, "Just so, I tell you, there will be more joy in heaven over one sinner who repents than over ninety-nine righteous persons who need no repentance." At the end of the lost coin story he says, "Just so, I tell you, there is joy in the presence of the angels of God over one sinner who repents." Suddenly, it seems, we have become the lost sheep and the lost coin. We may not have expected this role reversal, but our feelings tell us that it is true. When we have experienced a loss, it is we who feel that sense of lostness, that deep feeling of abandonment. We do become the lost ones who need to be found.

Perhaps we recognize just as suddenly the true identity of the shepherd and the woman. The one searching for the lost is none other than God. The good news, then, is that when we are in those lonely times of great loss, when we *feel* lost, God is looking for us. God's intention is not to magically replace what has been lost; rather, God is looking with open arms to embrace us, to welcome us home, to touch us with amazing grace, to do a work in us that goes beyond imagining.

It has been my own experience, and the experience of others whom I have known or read about, that God does some remarkable work in us at these times of loss. If we open our hearts to God, the moment can become a significant turning point. It was in the midst of losing my father, for instance, that I first sensed a call to the ministry. Sometime later, after seminary, just two years into ordained ministry, I had the feeling that I had already used up or lost every ounce of ministerial ability I ever had. For the most part I had given up on ever finding the right person to share my life with. Then I was called to a congregation that relit the fire in my soul, and I met the man who lit a fire in my heart as well.

Letting Go

A key factor in experiencing the miracle of recovery is learning to let go—the grace of acceptance. To accept a loss does not mean that we have to be happy about it. In fact, it is the moment of acceptance that usually brings tears. It is when we accept the fact of the loss that we begin to truly grieve. Accepting the loss really means that we accept the fact that we have a task to do. That task is to grieve. In the process our feelings range from numbness to intense sadness to anger and back again before the healing is complete.

I became very close to a woman in her early sixties who was a member of our former congregation in California. Virginia was a very intelligent woman with a great sense of humor. She was also an artist. I have two of her works hanging on the walls of our office. When Ed and I met her, she had just been diagnosed with Lou Gehrig's disease, a degenerative disease in which the muscles slowly atrophy while the mind remains as sharp and clear as ever. The end of the disease, for most victims, is suffocation. I watched as Virginia gradually lost the ability to speak clearly and eventually the ability to speak at all. When I visited her, I would talk and she would write notes. Pretty soon she couldn't swallow and had to receive nourishment through a tube in her stomach. She continued to lose her motor skills until even writing notes became almost impossible. Every week she came to a midweek prayer service that we held to ask God for healing. As I watched Virginia die by inches, it was frustrating to know that all I could do was pray and stand by her.

Her husband, Ed, always the practical one, found the strength to accept what was happening. At every stage he found ways to take the edge off her suffering. Their phone was set up to accommodate TDD services. He got a computer program that would speak from a typed message. At one point, he talked about selling their home and going into an "old soldiers' home" in order to pay for adequate care for Virgie. Each step was a wrenching struggle for Virginia because she thought that acceptance meant a lack of faith. And she wanted desperately to believe that God would heal her.

Stuart Briscoe describes a process often experienced by those who come to this life-and-death struggle. "When I talk with sick people," he says, "I see how much hope means to them. At first they hope nothing is wrong. When they discover that all is not well, they hope it is not serious. When that hope perishes, they hope something can be done, but if they are told eventually there is 'no hope,' I, as a Christian, can remind them that there is hope even if death cannot be avoided."[5]

As her health deteriorated, Virginia continued to paint as much as she was able. Finally she came to her last painting, and she knew it would be her last. A hospital chaplain had suggested that she paint her disease as a kind of therapy. I was struck by how this piece of work differed from her others. This one was dark and troubled looking, not calm and peaceful. It was a cave, with a dark, bowed figure inside. As she worked on the painting, she told me that the last thing she planned to paint was a cross overlaid on the other figures, signifying God's grace in the midst of this illness. She never got to paint that cross. I like to think that Jesus painted the last strokes for Virginia.

When we begin to understand the Holy Spirit's intercession for us, we begin also to be lifted out of our suffering, even though our suffering may well continue to the point of death, as it did for my friend Virginia. Being a Christian, a follower of Jesus Christ, does not insulate us from loss or from the pain of loss. But it gives us an avenue for genuine recovery, a spiritual renewal—the peace that passes understanding.

This peace is something that Chicago lawyer Horatio Spafford experienced in 1873.

> [He] placed his wife and four children on the luxury liner *Ville de Havre* sailing from New York to France. Spafford expected to join them in about three or four weeks after finishing up some business, but with the exception of his wife he never saw them again. The trip

started out beautifully. But on the evening of November 21, 1873, as the *Ville de Havre* proceeded peacefully across the Atlantic, the ship was suddenly struck by another vessel, the *Lochearn,* and sank a mere thirty minutes later, with the loss of nearly all on board.

On being told that the ship was sinking Mrs. Spafford knelt with her children and prayed that they might be saved or be made willing to die, if such was God's will. A few minutes later, in the confusion, three of the children were swept away by the waves while she stood clutching the youngest. Suddenly the youngest was swept from her arms. Mrs. Spafford became unconscious and awoke later to find that she had been rescued by sailors from the *Lochearn.* But her four children were gone.

Back in the United States, Horatio Spafford was waiting for news of his family and at last, ten days later (after the rescue ship had reached Cardiff), it came. "Saved alone" was his wife's message. That night Spafford walked the floor of his rooms in anguish, as anyone would have done. But this was not all. For as he shared his loss with his Lord, a loss that could not be reversed in this life, he found, as many have, that peace that indeed passes all understanding. Toward morning he told a friend named Major Whittle, "I am glad to be able to trust my Lord when it costs me something." Then, some time later, as he reflected on the disaster at sea, he wrote this hymn:

> When peace, like a river, attendeth my way,
> When sorrows like sea-billows roll;
> Whatever my lot, Thou has taught me to say,
> It is well, it is well with my soul.[6]

Interlude: Mad River

As I waded carefully upstream, casting my fly lightly onto the river, I breathed deeply. My eyes captured every ripple of the water, my ears every sound of scurrying wildlife. For the first time in two years—finally—I was in the middle of my preferred personal renewal activity: fly fishing. Hard as I tried, though, I couldn't shake a certain uncomfortable feeling. What was wrong? I wasn't catching fish, but that wasn't the problem. I have many "no fish" days in my fishing journal. If only I were fishing the Metolius, I would know what to do, I thought to myself. Green drakes would be hatching midafternoon, and I would be there. If no trout appeared, no matter. They would be there for me tomorrow. Today, I could just drink in the familiar beauty of the place and let God speak in the rush of the river.

But the Metolius was more than three thousand miles away. The scenery was unfamiliar, and the fish's favorite hiding spots unknown. And that was the problem, of course. A year and a half earlier Ed and I had moved from west to east to pastor a new church start. This was our first break of any length, fishing the Mad River in Vermont. As on other fishing vacations, we came to the Mad with a load of stress. And we looked to our time on the river for some healing and renewal. I wanted—I expected—the same kind of easy relationship that I had developed with the Metolius. Actually, I wanted it to *be* the Metolius. But it was clear from the first day that this new relationship was different. I couldn't simply walk the familiar paths and feel the familiar feelings. It takes time and effort to get acquainted with a new stream. What's hatching, and what hatches the fish like best. What time of day the best hatches happen and what holes the fish like to hide in.

Learning the twists and turns of the new river seemed too much like work. We discovered that instead of a midday hatch, the Mad trout vastly preferred the sunrise and sunset hatches—fishing times not all that compatible with a sleep-in vacation. Then there were the local residents we had to get used to—like the beaver I encountered one evening that was not at all pleased with my encroaching on his turf. With a slap of his tail he loudly announced to the neighborhood that a nefarious human was near. Whatever trout may have been in the vicinity vanished immediately.

If only I were at the Metolius, I kept thinking as the days went by. I just don't know this river. Then it occurred to me that this must be the kind of feeling people get when they have lost a long-term relationship with someone. It's tough to move on. Awkward. Everything's unfamiliar. Will this work? I was home-sick, of course, still grieving the loss of a sense of home that I felt at the Metolius. The river had been a source of real comfort and healing at some pretty significant times. But now the Metolius was inaccessible, at least for the time being. Time to move on.

Finally, we reached a compromise. Ed and I stopped forcing the unsuccessful midday fishing, and moved to sunset. The river gave up a few feisty rainbows and brookies. And we began to get acquainted with the Mad River, so named because it runs from south to north, unlike most rivers in the northern hemisphere, which run from north to south. A countercultural river, running its own course against the norm. An appropriate river for people who would care to spend a summer vacation at a ski resort (which is exactly what we were doing in Vermont). People whose lives take a course that diverges somewhat from the beaten path.

We reached an understanding, the Mad River and I, and found some common ground. Will the relationship last? Will the Mad become a second Metolius? Perhaps not. Some relationships are unique. Only time will tell. But it was a start.

CHAPTER 6

The Best Revenge

I once saw a sign in a counselor's office that read, "Living well is the best revenge." How tempting it is, when life dishes out its worst, to harbor grudges and nurture bitterness, to turn inward and become self-protective. Yet in the end, these strategies, instead of protecting us against further onslaughts, turn on us and bring us harm. It is much better, in the *kairos* moments of life, to turn to God, who is able to heal and forgive—who is even able to enable us to forgive. To turn to God in these moments is to live well. In this chapter we will consider the marks of a life lived well, some indicators that our journey, though often stumbling, is headed in the right direction.

A Good Memory

Each year, when Ed and I open our box of Christmas decorations and begin taking out the familiar ornaments, something else begins to tumble out of the big box as well—memories. In many ways, our Christmas decorations are a storehouse of memories. We bought a special ornament for the tree the year we were married to add to the ornaments that I had already collected. Every year since, we have added one special ornament that in some way captures where we were living or what was happening in our lives at the time: a puffin from Alaska, a Canada goose from Oregon, a mailbox the year we moved into our house in New Jersey, a ceramic figure of a graduate the year Ed finished his dissertation for the doctor of ministry degree.

Memories are a big part of Christmas. Have you noticed how many conversations at Christmastime begin with "I remember"? I remember lutefisk and lefse for supper on Christmas Eve. I remember my mom and dad piling all of us kids into the old Ford and driving twelve miles to the old country church. I remember the crunch of the snow under the tires, the bite of the north wind, and the brilliance of the stars in the dark Dakota sky. I remember coming home from church and sitting around our ancient oak table and opening our gifts one by one—and how my brother used to drive the rest of us crazy by carefully and slowly slitting the tape on each of his presents with a pocket knife. I remember the first Christmas after my dad died and how we all felt because of the empty place at the table. I remember too the first Christmas that I spent alone in Seattle. And the first Christmas Ed and I spent together. Then there was the Christmas when Ramey, our middle dog, got impatient and started unwrapping the presents under the tree.

A precious thing that God restores in the turning points is our memory. When we are no longer afraid to face the past or what people have done to us, or what the future may hold, our memory begins to be healed. A loss of memory is a part of the addictive process. Addicts of all kinds, including codependents, tend to have bad memories. It's a part of the denial system. For those who have been abused, a loss of memory is often a coping mechanism. It's a way of buffering the pain. Some people literally forget their abuse for years, until another trauma occurs or a loving friend or therapist pries the memory loose. Just as surgery is the painful but necessary solution to many physical maladies, the restoration of painful memories is often the beginning of a journey to wholeness.

The healing of our memory is good for our spiritual life as well as our emotional life because believing is an act of memory. That statement may sound strange to you, but consider the depth of meaning that the word "remember" conveys. In the Bible the word "remember" refers to more than just a mental exercise, such as "do you remember what year Columbus sailed to America?" That's one kind of remembering—remembering facts. But the kind of remembering that the Bible talks about is more like "did you remember to take out the garbage?" or "did you remember to turn off the coffee pot?" In the Bible, remembering isn't just thinking about something, it's doing something.

For example, in Genesis 8, it is said that God remembered Noah. At the time, Noah and his family and a horde of smelly animals were trapped in a big boat in the middle of a rainstorm that just wouldn't quit. And when God remembered Noah, the Bible says that the winds began to subside, the boat settled down on dry land, and everybody got out. Thank goodness God remembered!

"Remember Jesus Christ," Paul said to his young friend Timothy (2 Timothy 2:8). "Do this in remembrance of me," Jesus said at his last Passover with the disciples (Luke 22:19). Remember Jesus Christ. What does it mean to remember Jesus Christ? For a Christian, to remember means to live life under the authority of the gospel of Jesus Christ, to live a life that is consistent with our confession that Jesus is Lord. It means to live up to the promises and commitments that we have made. It means to grow and to change in the ways that God leads us. In the early church, when people lost their faith or left the church, they were described as having amnesia. They didn't remember anymore. Memory is crucial to living the Christian faith.

During his farewell speech to the Israelites, shortly before his death and before their entrance into the Promised Land, Moses cautioned the people about prosperous times to come when they would be settled in their own land and would be wealthier than they could imagine. "Take care," Moses said, "that you do not forget the LORD, who brought you out of the land of Egypt, out of the house of slavery" (Deuteronomy 6:12). But they did forget, again and again.

In those restless years between the Exodus and the establishment of the kingdom of Israel, the Israelites followed a cycle of turning away from God and then turning back in repentance. In 1 Samuel 7, the writer describes one of these episodes. Samuel challenged the people to turn away from false gods and turn once again to the Lord. They did, and then the Philistines launched an attack against them. But "the LORD thundered with a mighty voice that day against the Philistines and threw them into confusion" (1 Samuel 7:10), and so the Israelites won. Many times we feel like these Old Testament stories full of violence and bloodshed are unrelated to our own lives. But we *do* have our own battles to deal with, don't we? What God wants of us is the same as what God wanted from the children of Israel: to trust God no matter what the battle.

It seems that whenever things were going well for Israel, the people forgot about God. They settled in and absorbed the easy and seductive ways of the people around them. They forgot what God had done for them. This is precisely what we do as well. We cry out to God when we come under attack in some area of our lives. But when things settle down, we have a tendency to go our own way and forget about God. After the battle with the Philistines, the prophet Samuel set up a stone in a prominent location and named it Ebenezer (which means "stone of help") and said, "Thus far the LORD has helped us." (1 Samuel 7:12). It was a reminder to the Israelites that they had not won the battle on their own.

It's helpful for us to set up some Ebenezers of our own to act as signposts that mark the places where God has helped us, marking the steps of our journey as we dance and stumble from one turning point to the next, blazing a trail to the future that God has for us. For some of us, this means a journal or a prayer diary, chronicling our journey with God. For others, it means telling their story. In my study at home I have two pictures of Jesus. Both are very contemporary depictions. In one he is praying and in the other, laughing. When things are going well, the prayerful one reminds me to pray. When I am struggling, the other one reminds me that the future is hopeful.

Many of the things we do in our churches are designed to help us remember. We approach the Lord's Table, the Eucharist, for instance, to remember what Jesus has done—to remember the extent to which he has loved us. The songs that we sing, the prayers that we pray, and the symbols that we use are all reminders of who we are in God's sight. They are Ebenezers that say, "Thus far the LORD has helped us." Thanks be to God!

Learning to Count Our Blessings

Several years ago, Ed and I and our three Labradors spent two weeks at a house on the northern Oregon coast, in the little town of Gearhardt. I woke up the first morning feeling a deep sense of restfulness and security and peace—I felt happy in a sense that I had not felt for quite some time. It reminded me of the feeling I used to get as a kid, when I would wake up on a Saturday morning with the weekend ahead of me and no homework. There is something about the ocean that promotes a sense of well-being, that gives permission to just *be* for a while. Something about the endless roar of the surf, the faint mist that always hangs just above the water, the breeze that is usually blowing clouds in or out, the cool, moist air. At that moment in time, it was just what my soul and body needed, and it felt like a gift from God.

Perhaps you have a place or a time when you've had that feeling as well. Maybe the memory of it can bring back a hint of the feeling. This sense of well-being comes awfully close to the definition of the biblical word *blessed*. In biblical terms, to be blessed is to be happy, to have a sense of well-being. Another definition is to be free from daily cares and worries. That certainly describes the feeling I had when I woke up on that particularly restful morning at the beach. Although I was there to write and study, I was free from the daily cares and worries that regularly assailed me in the office. And that is a blessed state of being.

A blessing is a gift from God that results in this sense of well-being. In the Bible, there is always a "God connection" with the notion of blessing. Another sign of a life that is learning to turn to God is the ability to count one's blessings. The Bible guides us in our understanding of how to do this. In the earliest writings of the Bible, the way to count blessings was to count your material possessions, your health, your family. Do you have a large family, many children, much cattle, many servants, a lot of money, and good health? Then you are blessed by God. A good example is the story of Jacob and his father-in-law, Laban. While Jacob has been with Laban, serving him to earn his two wives (Rachel and Leah), Laban's net worth has skyrocketed. Laban acknowledges this, when he says, "The LORD has blessed me because of you." Jacob responds, "You yourself know how I have served you, and how your cattle have fared with me. For you had little before I came, and it has increased abundantly; and the LORD has blessed you wherever I turned." (See Genesis 30:27-30.)

One way, then, to count our blessings is to count up all the things we have and to acknowledge that they are gifts from God. Ed and I have become accustomed to counting our material blessings in terms of pounds, due to our many moves. On one move we "counted" sixty-five hundred pounds of household goods and another thousand pounds of books. A few years ago, though, we counted our blessings in a slightly different way, by writing our will. We had to list all our assets, at least in general terms. In monetary terms, our most valuable asset is our life insurance. Our house has a great deal of monetary value, but we owe most of that back to the bank. From a professional standpoint, our most valuable asset is our library. From a personal standpoint, the possessions carrying the greatest value are our three dogs. More important still are those things that are not our "possessions" at all—family and friends, a sunset, a sunrise. Our material blessings are gifts from God. And one way to thank God is to stand back and count the things God has given. But we need to remember that material possessions are not everything, even as we give thanks for them. Otherwise, our attitude toward them can become bent and twisted, thinking that these things actually bring us happiness. Then we base our lives on the bumper-sticker motto: The one with the most toys at the end wins. This is the motto of those who have stopped counting *blessings* and have in effect counted God out of their lives—they are only counting things. Remember, there is always a "God connection" when it comes to blessings. We know that it is not *things* that bring us into a state of blessedness. It is our relationship with God.

What if our list of material possessions is short, or what if we suddenly lose everything? Then we may tend to feel that God has not blessed us very much. The consumeristic culture that we live in encourages us to focus on what we lack, of course (always reminding us that we need to acquire more). It does not encourage us to remember the great blessings we have, since that would promote a sense of contentment and discourage further consumption. But it's good to remember Saint Augustine's great saying: "Thou hast made us for thyself, O God, and our hearts are restless until they rest in thee." Those who count only *things* as blessings tend to become increasingly restless, bitter, self-protective, and greedy. Far from feeling a sense of blessedness, they are most often very unhappy.

Again, it is in the turning points that we begin to understand this. Our priorities shift. I think the key is to count our possessions as blessings from God, but to hold them rather loosely. And to count our relationship with God as our greatest blessing and to hold on to that relationship very tightly, lest we become like the rich young man whom Jesus called. The man was unable to turn from his material blessings in order to follow God.

It's interesting to notice that as the Old Testament progresses, there is a shift in the kinds of blessings that are counted by the biblical writers. While in the early writings, it was material goods, later writings suggest that the highest blessing from God is wisdom. Solomon, the great and wealthy king of Israel, asked for one thing from God: wisdom. Sometimes wisdom is perceived as a "high falutin'" and philosophical thing, but it's not. Wisdom is very pragmatic. It is the knowledge of how to live well, how to make good decisions, and how to know right from wrong and apply that knowledge to real life. Wisdom enables us to make good decisions; it tells us when to speak and when to keep our mouths shut; when we should listen to new ideas and when we should hold our course steady. Solomon is known for wise decisions. Probably everyone has heard about a certain disagreement that was brought before him. Two women claimed the same baby, so Solomon commanded that the child be cut in half. Immediately one woman objected and insisted that the other woman take the child. The woman who cried out was awarded the child because Solomon knew that the real mother would rather give up the child than see it cut in half.

In the New Testament, Jesus turns the idea of blessings inside out, going beyond material blessings, beyond the blessings of wisdom, when he insists that the poor in spirit, the meek, and those who mourn are blessed. Those whom we might have pitied turn out to be ones who need to count their blessings. It seems backward, and it requires a transformed attitude (the fruit of many turning points) to even begin to grasp how it is that people in such circumstances could be called blessed. Yet if we have learned to turn to God in all circumstances of life, we will recognize that it is not the negative circumstances that create the state of blessedness any more than it is the positive ones. It is the presence of God, which transforms our hearts. We may well ask what connections exist between material blessings, the blessing of wisdom, and the blessing of a transformed attitude reflected in the beatitudes. Throughout Scripture we find a connecting thread. That connection is God's intervention in people's lives.

Counting blessings, then, is not just counting, it's recounting—telling about—those times when God entered into our lives to bring us hope. When you read the Bible with this in mind, you will be amazed at how many times the stories of God's intervention are told and retold. Psalm 136 is one great example. It tells about God's intervention in the world from the creation to the Exodus. The Exodus story is one that is told again and again in the Bible, to remind people of what God has done. Individuals can do this as well. The apostle Paul is a good example. He loved to tell what God had done in his life—how God had entered into his life with great power and drama, turning him around, providing for his needs, and giving him direction (Acts 26 is one example). My Exodus story, the one I tell with similar repetitiveness, is my call to ministry and God's miraculous provision for me. This occasion was the first time I was genuinely aware of God's power to move me (both geographically and emotionally).

It is God's intervention in people's lives that turns history into what theologians call holy history or salvation history (which is what the history of the Bible is called). Telling our own story helps us to recount our blessings and to see what God has done. Thus far the Lord has helped us. Thanks be to God!

Beyond the Verge

Many people live life "on the verge." Tomorrow I will stop smoking, next month I will lose some weight. When the kids go off to college, I will take more time for myself or we'll work on our marriage. I know I ought to spend more time reading the Bible and praying, but I am just too busy right now. I'll do that later. We see other people making significant decisions about their lives, experiencing emotional and spiritual healing, and we applaud them. But it doesn't touch us—not yet. We wonder, in our honest moments, will it ever? Will I ever slow down enough, get real enough, to face the turning points in my own life? Yet we are haunted by a sense that things somehow need to be different, need to be better.

In John 5, we are told about a man who had been ill for thirty-eight years. He spent his waking hours by a pool of water in Jerusalem that was called Bethzatha (or Bethesda). He and countless other invalids lay by the pool, waiting for the slightest ripple in the water, which, according to local legend, meant that an angel of healing was stirring up the water. Also according to legend, the first one into the water at such moments was healed. Our man by the pool was dependent on the help of others to lower him into the pool, and in his own words, "I have no one to put me into the pool when the water is stirred up; and while I am making my way, someone else steps down ahead of me" (John 5:7).

Because he never makes it into the supposedly healing waters, he remains immersed in his disease, withdrawn from life and staring at the mesmerizing water that he can never hope to reach. Then Jesus touches him on the shoulder. He says, "Do you want to be made well?" His answer to Jesus' question amounts to a rationalization of why he is still disabled.

He is so much like us. Our hurts are real, no question about it. And Jesus asks us the same question: "Do you want to be made well? Or do you want to keep staring, paralyzed, into a pool of despair?" How many times do people say tacitly, through their actions, "No, I guess I really don't want to be made well." How many times, when people need the fellowship and the healing of the church the most, they stay away! Have we given the impression that the church is a fortress for those who "have it made" instead of a haven for sinners and sick people and those who are hurting? Or are people unwilling to be touched and changed?

As we answer "yes, I want to be made well, yes, I want to live into this turning point," we will find ourselves moving beyond the verge, not to a magical pool but into the loving arms of Jesus. And into life. We will be willing to be vulnerable again, willing to risk again.

Back when Alexander the Great was leading his army on military campaigns throughout the known world, there seemed to be a shortage of maps. It's not that there were too few maps, but that some parts of the world had not yet been charted. And I am told that "consternation . . . came upon the Greek army as it followed Alexander across Asia Minor when they discovered they had marched clear off the map. The only maps they had showed only a portion of Asia Minor. The rest was a blank space and they filled it in as they went along. Their maps told them where they had been [but] not where they were going."[1]

It can be scary traveling without a map. Yet if we look at the lives of those who have accomplished great things, a common thread is that these people have been willing to go beyond the comfort zone of their old experience and even beyond the known maps into uncharted territory. One characteristic of the life lived well is the willingness to risk.

I want to be clear about the kind of risk that I'm talking about because we take all kinds of risks in life for all kinds of reasons, from going over Niagara Falls in a barrel to taking psychedelic drugs to investing in real estate. Some take risks for thrill and publicity or perhaps to fill an emptiness inside, while others take a risk in the present in order to make the future less risky.

The kind of risk that I am talking about is not quite like any of the ones just mentioned—not risking for the thrill of it (though there will be some thrills along the way), nor for what we can get out of it in the long run (though we will receive much). The kind of risk that I am talking about is the risk that is synonymous with the word "faith." It means to be so confident in God's call that we are willing to take great risks to accomplish it, even if it means walking right off the map. The kind of risk, for instance, that a young man named Joseph took. He had a solid business, and he was engaged to a beautiful young woman. He had life pretty much figured out until Mary came to him and said, "I'm pregnant." He knew that he was not the baby's father, and he was a moral man, so his first inclination was to break off the engagement. But he loved Mary, and he listened to a voice telling him it would be OK. He took the risk, married his fiancée, stepped off the familiar map of his experience, and became a part of God's great drama of salvation history.

Abraham and Sarah took similar risks. So did Moses, David, Solomon, Esther, Deborah, Elijah, Matthew, James, Peter, Mary of Bethany, Priscilla and Aquila, and Paul. And Martin Luther, John Wesley, John Calvin, Martin Luther King Jr. These are people whose accomplishments could not have been achieved if they had not taken great risks in order to respond to God's call in their lives.

Elizabeth O'Connor, of the Church of the Savior in Washington, D.C., says that God's call involves risk more often than not, and "often does not seem very prudent to those looking on. A journey is also involved. Call asks that we set out from a place that is familiar and relatively secure for a destination that can be only dimly perceived, and that we cannot be at all certain of reaching, so many are the obstacles that will loom along the way."[2]

Indeed, our journey of faith may look foolish to those looking on, but faith is not foolish at all to those who possess it. To them, faith "is the assurance of things hoped for, the conviction of things not seen" (Hebrews 11:1). It is by faith, then, that we step off our known map and enter into what God is doing in our world. It is by faith that God's power is set loose in our midst and into the world.

By faith Noah, by faith Abraham, by faith Sarah, by faith Enoch and Abel and Rahab and all the rest. By faith each one walked off the map of known experience into the strong hands of God. From time to time, God has called me to take such a step. The first was my "exodus" from rural South Dakota to southern California, which was just the beginning of a life of off-the-map experiences for me. The scariest one to date was when I walked down the aisle and repeated "till death do us part." What could be more frightening than to make a pledge for life? Am I up to it? Is he? More recently a turning point brought Ed and me from California to New Jersey.

No matter how many times God has called me to take that kind of risk, it has never been easy. It always feels risky, but when it is God's call, there is always something else present as well: the rock-solid assurance of things hoped for, the certainty based on a tested and tried relationship with our powerful God. Thus far the Lord has helped us. Thanks be to God!

Laughter

Earlier, I described my family's reluctance to express feelings. We didn't think that it was OK to feel too good or too bad about anything, but one type of expression, laughter, was acceptable, as long as you didn't do it in some "inappropriate" place (like church). I remember sitting around our big round oak table on a Friday night playing games and eating popcorn, and somebody would start to laugh: a giggle or a snort at something inane that somebody said or did. Pretty soon the table would shake with our laughter. And this laughter was not limited to my immediate family. We shared the same kind of laughter when all my aunts, uncles, and cousins would get together. One of my uncles (by marriage) used to say we couldn't see each other without having "a good old Jacobson laugh."

Laughter is good for the soul, and some people even claim that it can cure cancer. Laughter is in my blood, and when I go for extended periods without it, I know something is dreadfully wrong. My current ministry is a place where laughter is prized. Much the better, other feelings are welcomed as well. Our Wednesday evening music rehearsals ordinarily turn into laugh therapy sessions. Sometimes Bible studies do too. And, yes, we laugh in church on Sunday mornings. A lot.

The first church I served, in Seattle, Washington, had more than its share of jokesters. That characteristic helped me through many of the mistakes I made as well as the prejudice against "woman pastors" that I encountered. One of the elders, whom I had occasion to call at his business from time to time, told me that his secretary had handed him a phone message that "a lady named Myrlene called." George replied, "That's no lady! That's the preacher." On another occasion, I was preparing for a pulpit exchange with another congregation. One of the women came to me wearing a look of mock seriousness. "I just don't know how we'll feel about having a MAN in the pulpit!"

These were the same people who said that they really didn't care if my sermons were boring because just behind the pulpit was a giant picture window overlooking Lake Washington. On Pentecost Sunday, when I had encouraged everyone to wear red, the liturgical color of the day, one of the elders came dressed in a Hawaiian shirt that was neon pink, orange, and red. He walked in late with his wife, and as they sat down in the front row, a wide grin lit up his face and his shoulders were shaking with laughter.

My preaching robe is a long white alb, cinched at the waist with a rope. One of the kids asked his mom if I was so poor that I couldn't afford a belt. She assured him that I could buy a belt if I wanted to.

Where do you go to find laughter that is good for your soul? Perhaps if you look hard enough, you can find it in your own story. Did you ever think of looking in the Bible? It's there too. My favorite biblical sitcom is the one starring Abraham and Sarah, which I have described at some length elsewhere.[3] God has some pretty lofty plans for Abraham and Sarah. They are somehow involved in God's plan of salvation for the whole world—a plan that stretches over centuries of time and culminates in Jesus Christ, and it all hinges on one thing: Abraham and Sarah's son. But Sarah is barren. Through a series of tragic/comic events, ultimately God makes good on the promise, and the child is named "Laughter" (Isaac).

Perhaps you are familiar with some of Jesus' jokes. The most famous is the one about the camel and the needle. It was like one of Johnny Carson's "how hard is it?" jokes. Jesus begins, "It is so hard for a rich person to enter the kingdom of heaven." [How hard is it?] "It's so hard that it's easier for a camel to go through the eye of a needle than is for a rich person to get into the kingdom of heaven." Not long ago I heard a contemporary version: that it's easier to suck a John Deere tractor through a straw. This is outrageous humor! It's so outrageous that people try to soften it, try to think of other things that Jesus must have meant other than a literal needle or an actual camel. But that's the point. It is outrageous to think that anyone can get into the kingdom of heaven on personal merit. The disciples don't get the joke. "Then how can anyone be saved?" they gasp. They thought rich people had a leg up as far as getting into the kingdom was concerned. (Now Jesus has the audience in the palm of his hand for the real punch line.) Well, with people it *is* impossible, but not with God. (See Luke 18:24-26.)

Luke shows his own flair for humor when just a few paragraphs later, a camel does go through the eye of the needle, as Zacchaeus, a sinfully rich and contemptibly wicked tax collector, is converted.

The people of God need laughter. Not a giggle or a few snorts, but a good belly laugh that expresses a depth of joy that is almost inexpressible. And certainly irrepressible. Such laughter is the "aha!" of the soul. It's an expression of faith that says, Now I get it. Thus far the Lord has helped us. Thanks be to God!

Love

Another mark of a life lived well is a thing called "love." Most of us have a lot of misinformation about what love is, much of it coming from Madison Avenue and Hollywood. If we buy the right toothpaste or the powerful mouthwash, we will find love. Assuming the toothpaste and mouthwash bring us love, what kind of love is it that we have found? Sex? Sentimentalism? A feeling that is here today and gone tomorrow? A "nice" relationship? An idea made popular some years ago by the movie *Love Story* was "love means never having to say you're sorry." That might be true if we were perfect and psychic, always knowing, always doing what pleases our spouse or loved one, but this is not the real world. In the real world we make mistakes. In the real world, we hurt each other.

Those in addictive or dysfunctional families also get a skewed education on love. In that context, "love" often means protecting and covering up for the addict. Or love means controlling people's behavior "for their own good." An elderly woman in a former congregation expressed her love through food, mostly chocolate chip cookies, which she brought to every committee meeting at the church. She often brought some especially for Ed and me. The problem was that it got to be a bit much. Ed was on a diet, no cookies allowed. I have a small appetite, though I love chocolate chip cookies. Soon this crusader of love began bringing home-made casseroles, cherry cheesecake, and pumpkin pie. Since she seemed to enjoy doing this so much, we accepted her gifts to be nice. She was in many ways a lonely woman. Her husband had died years earlier, and her only child, a son, lived some distance away. What could it hurt to accept a few gifts? When I broke my leg, the food deliveries increased. When food started getting fuzzy in our refrigerator, we tried to refuse her offers. She brought the food anyway. She loved us, she said, but it was getting to the point where we couldn't plan our own meals. It felt like a battle. Finally we had to stop being "nice" and start being truthful. The food had to stop. Even so, it was tough to untangle ourselves from the food without hurting the giver. I'm not sure we succeeded.

An opposite and equally devastating misuse of "love" occurs when someone announces, "I'm telling you this in love" and then clobbers you over the head with some outrageous criticism.

I believe that as we turn to God in the *kairos* moments of our lives, we begin to learn what true love is and begin to be able to truly love. A*gape*, the kind of love that God gives us, rubs off on our relationships. The more we get to know God, the more we discover that love is both tender and tough. It is the prophet Hosea forgiving his unfaithful wife (a picture of God's forgiveness toward wayward people). It is Jesus wrapping his arms around little children. And it is the same Jesus taking a whip into the temple courtyard, shaking his fist at Pharisees, and telling Peter to "get behind me, Satan." It is the same Jesus going to the cross because of his love for the world.

A person who loves with *agape* love is willing to lay down her life for the one loved; still, the lover has boundaries and does not allow someone else's unhealthy needs to direct her away from her own call or her own principles. To give *agape* love to someone means to genuinely wish God's best for him or her (which may involve healing, recovery, growth—processes that often involve pain). It does not mean being a doormat.

When an elderly woman's husband died, her will to live died too. He had been her best friend, and he apparently had enabled her to maintain her alcoholism. Her family cared deeply for her and recognized that if she didn't get help for her addiction, she would die, most likely by her own hand. One of her relatives commented, "She tried to get me to replace my uncle, to do all the financial work related to the estate, so that she could be free to keep drinking. I told her that what she really needed was help for her alcoholism, and then I left." A loving response? Yes, though not a "nice" one. Interestingly, I once checked my concordance for the word "nice" and found that it is not in the Bible, at least not in any of the translations that I own. We are called to be faithful, kind, loving, truthful, but not once are we commanded to be "nice." That's an idea we created to avoid being honest. When I spoke about this in a small group recently, one young woman commented that in many contexts we have gone so far as to equate "nice" with "Christian"—as in, "that's not a Christian thing to say," when we *mean* "that's not a nice thing to say." "Nice" and "Christian" are not synonyms! Sometimes the two ideas are compatible, but not always. As my friend pointed out, we need to learn the difference.

Kathleen Norris talks about the habit of "making nice" that both people in small towns and people in churches seem to have:

> Why risk discussion that might cause unpleasantness? I was once at a pastor search committee meeting when a woman said, "We don't want anyone too old." A pastor from a neighboring town who was guiding us through the bureaucratic thickets, a woman who had been ordained the week of her sixty-fifth birthday, said, amicably but

firmly, "I know most churches feel that way, but maybe you should think about that." Another woman jumped in and said, "Oh, we didn't mean anything. It was all in fun." The bluntness of the first woman was at least useful; had she been more urbane, she would have disguised her prejudice. But the lie put forth by the other woman was intended to silence us. Thanks to the minister's persistence, we did manage a brief look at the question of what age we wanted our next pastor to be, but it was painful. Among other things, it forced us to look at the fact that our congregation is aging, and people wanted to drop the subject as quickly as possible.[4]

One of Jesus' last commandments to his disciples was to "love one another. Just as I have loved you, you also should love one another" (John 13:34). This commandment is a tall order, one that we can only do by the power at work within us, but thus far the Lord has helped us. Thanks be to God!

Epilogue

When I was growing up on the farm, one of my favorite pastimes was rock hunting. As I walked the pastures and fields, inevitably I would find an agate or piece of quartz or petrified wood and stick it in my pocket. A few of my favorites have traveled with me in my nomadic journey throughout the country. Over the years, I would bring them out from time to time and just look at them, remembering. Just before Christmas last year, I put a rock tumbler on my wish list. Ed was puzzled, but he complied. Since then, I have been tumbling load after load of childhood rocks, local rocks, and any other rocks that pique my interest.

What intrigues me about the tumbling process is that the result is often a surprise. Sometimes the rocks that come out of the tumbler bear almost no resemblance to the rocks that I put in. They have colors and a shine that I would not have suspected. Others are disappointing. They require two or three or extra cycles to even begin to smooth out enough to take a good polish. The process itself is a lesson in patience. From start to finish, polishing takes about a month. The instant-gratification-craving baby boomer in me almost goes berserk sometimes waiting to see the results of my tumbling. The tumbler is in our crawl space, and if I put my ear to the heat vents I can hear the gentle rumble of stone rolling over stone, but even when I go down into the crawl space and watch, I can't see anything but the outside of the tumbler, just going around and around and around. It's like the caterpillar all wrapped up in its cocoon. On the outside nothing appears to be happening, but on the inside, beauty is being born. The instructions to the tumbler give a stern warning not to let the tumbler sit idle in the middle of a cycle because the grit (which is mixed with water) will set up like cement if it sits still too long.

So it is with the polishing process called recovery. Troublesome rocks have accompanied many of us into adulthood: addiction rocks, codependence rocks, shame rocks, hurt rocks. One day we decide it's time to do something, and we get up the nerve to put some of them in God's tumbler. The results are much like what happens in my rock tumbler. There are surprises and disappointments, and it takes a long time (a lifetime). In some cases, we are greatly surprised at what God is able to do in us—what healing, what strengthening, what amazing changes, what astounding beauty we didn't know we had in us. In other cases we are disappointed because one cycle through the spiritual tumbler is not nearly enough. The process wears on our patience.

The lesson of the rock tumbler is this: keep on turning. If we stop the process midstream, we may well find we have become hard and rigid instead of healed. It is in the turning that we continue our growth.

When I was young, I had a fantasy about being "grown up." I thought it meant that there was a time somewhere out there, when the "growing" would be complete and from there on, I could just set the cruise control and relax. I suppose that came from reading so many fantasies that ended with "and they lived happily ever after." It may even have been mingled with such thoughts as "when I was a child, I spoke like a child, I thought like a child, I reasoned like a child; when I became an adult, I put an end to childish ways" (1 Corinthians 13:11). This could be interpreted to mean that adults have arrived. They have it all figured out (or ought to). Now I know that maturity does not mean being grown up; it means continuing to grow. As I pointed out earlier, each stage of life, from birth to death, has its own struggles and its own turning points. At each stage of life, as we turn to God, we continue to grow in faith.

Keep on turning. Don't believe the illusion that reading this book (or even applying its principles) means that you have "made it" spiritually or emotionally. Old patterns may reemerge. Old addictions or habits of thinking may continue to dog your steps. Old hurts that you thought were healed may start to bleed again. I know this because it is true for me and for the best of God's people.

Do not lose heart. Go back to the Old Testament and reread the stories about David (the whole story), about Abraham and Sarah (again, the whole story, not just the fun parts), about the children of Israel throughout the books of 1-2 Samuel, 1-2 Kings, and 1-2 Chronicles. Rediscover the humanness and the fallibility of the people whose life stories made it into the Bible. Then turn again to the God who gives grace upon grace and whose mercy provides the firm foundation for each turning point.

As you continue your journey toward wholeness, I wish for you a grace-ful persistence, knowing that the One "who began a good work in you will bring it to completion" (Philippians 1:6 RSV).

Notes

Chapter 1

1. Richard Chenevix Trench, *Synonyms of the New Testament* (Grand Rapids, Mich.: Eerdmans, 1953), 211.

2. Alan Richardson, ed., *A Theological Word Book of the Bible* (New York: Macmillan, 1950), 191.

3. Eugenia A. Gamble, "A Theology of Change for Spiritual Leaders," *Vanguard* 29, no. 2 (March 1992): 7-8.

4. C. S. Lewis, *The Problem of Pain* (New York: Macmillan, Collier Books, 1962), 115.

Chapter 2

1. Dietrich Bonhoeffer, *The Cost of Discipleship*, rev. ed. (New York: Macmillan Paperbacks, 1963), 62-63.

2. Richardson, *Theological Word Book*, 254.

3. Colin Brown, ed., *The New International Dictionary of New Testament Theology*, vol. 3 (Grand Rapids, Mich.: Zondervan, 1978), 818.

4. Ibid., 819.

5. Fanny J. Crosby, "All the Way My Savior Leads Me," 1875.

Chapter 3

1. Margery Williams, *The Velveteen Rabbit or, How Toys Become Real* (Philadelphia: Running Press, 1989), 18-24. Reprinted with permission from Running Press.

2. M. Scott Peck, *The Road Less Traveled: A New Psychology of Love, Traditional Values, and Spiritual Growth* (New York: Simon and Schuster, 1978), 15.

3. "Tara," quoted in "On the Rocks: Is Your Child Drinking behind Your Back?" by Sondra Forsyth, *Family Circle,* 5 April 1994, 86.

4. Leith Anderson, *Dying for Change* (Minneapolis: Bethany House, 1990), 84.

5. Melody Beattie, *Codependent No More: How to Stop Controlling Others and Start Caring for Yourself* (San Francisco: Harper and Row, 1987), 32.

6. Robert Hemfelt, Frank Minirth, and Paul Meier, *Love Is a Choice* (Nashville: Thomas Nelson, 1989), 15.

7. Virginia Curran Hoffman, *The Codependent Church* (New York: Crossroad, 1991), 15.

8. Robert Subby, quoted in *The Codependent Church,* 18-19.

9. Hoffman, *The Codependent Church,* 23.

10. Lewis B. Smedes, *Shame and Grace: Healing the Shame We Don't Deserve* (San Francisco: HarperCollins, 1993), 5.

11. Henry Cloud and John Townsend, *False Assumptions* (Grand Rapids, Mich.: Zondervan, 1994), 93-94.

12. Lewis Smedes, *Forgive and Forget* (San Francisco: Harper and Row, 1984), xii.

13. Corrie ten Boom, *Tramp for the Lord* (Old Tappan, N.J.: Fleming H. Revell, 1974), 55.

14. Lewis Smedes, *Forgive and Forget.*

Chapter 4

1. George Barna, *The Frog in the Kettle: What Christians Need to Know about Life in the Year 2000* (Ventura: Regal Books, 1990), 159.

2. Abraham Twerski, *Addictive Thinking: Understanding Self-Deception* (New York: HarperCollins, 1990), 9-10.

3. C. Austin Miles, "A New Name in Glory," 1910.

4. Cloud and Townsend, *False Assumptions,* 21.

5. Dorotheus of Gaza, quoted in *Dakota: A Spiritual*

Geography, by Kathleen Norris (New York: Houghton Mifflin, 1993), 174.

6. Bruce Larson, "None of Us Are Sinners Emeritus," *D. Min. News Network* 3, no. 1 (winter 1995): 2.

7. Anne Wilson Schaef and Diane Fassel, *The Addictive Organization* (San Francisco: Harper and Row, 1988), 50.

8. Pat Means, "Life beyond J-O-Y," *STEPS* 6, no. 3 (summer 1995): 17.

9. Henry Cloud and John Townsend, *Boundaries: When to Say Yes, When to Say No to Take Control of Your Life* (Grand Rapids: Zondervan, 1992), 31.

10. Ibid., 27-28.

11. Dale O. Wolery, "To Our Readers," *STEPS* 6, no. 3 (summer 1995): 3.

Chapter 5

1. Karl Barth, *The Epistle to the Romans,* trans. Edwyn C. Hoskins (London: Oxford University Press, 1968), 320.

2. C. S. Lewis, *Mere Christianity* (New York: Macmillan Paperbacks, 1960), 174.

3. Judith Viorst, *Necessary Losses* (New York: Simon and Schuster, 1986), 16.

4. Ibid.

5. D. Stuart Briscoe, *Romans,* The Communicator's Commentary series, Lloyd J. Oglvie, ed. (Waco, Tex.: Word, 1982), 6: 113.

6. James S. Hewett, ed., *Illustrations Unlimited* (Wheaton, Ill.: Tyndale, 1988), 243.

Chapter 6

1. Ken Miller, quoted in *The Pastor's Story File* 5, no. 3 (January 1989): 3.

2. Elizabeth O'Connor, *Cry Pain, Cry Hope: Thresholds to Purpose* (Waco, Tex.: Word, 1987), 82.

3. See my book, *Being the Body of Christ: A Handbook for Mobilizing Your Congregation* (Valley Forge, Pa.: Judson Press, 1994), 36-41.

4. Norris, *Dakota,* 81-82.

Helpful Resources for Christian Growth and Recovery

Books

Allender, D. *The Wounded Heart: Hope for Adult Victims of Childhood Sexual Abuse.* Colorado Springs, Colo.: NavPress, 1990.

Anderson, Ray. *The Gospel According to Judas.* Colorado Springs, Colo.: Helmers and Howard, 1991.

Arterburn, S., and J. Felton. *Toxic Faith.* Nashville: Thomas Nelson, 1991.

Beattie, Melody. *Codependent No More: How to Stop Controlling Others and Start Caring for Yourself.* San Francisco: Harper and Row, 1987.

———. *Beyond Codependency: And Getting Better All the Time.* San Francisco: Harper and Row, 1989.

———. *Codependents' Guide to the Twelve Steps: How to Find the Right Program for You and Apply Each of the Twelve Steps to Your Own Issues.* New York: Prentice-Hall/Parkside, 1992.

Berry, C. *When Helping You Is Hurting Me: Escaping the Messiah Trap.* New York: HarperCollins, 1988.

Carnes, Patrick. *Out of the Shadows: Understanding Sexual Addiction.* Minneapolis: CompCare Publishers, 1992.

Cloud, Henry, and John Townsend. *Boundaries: When to Say Yes,*

When to Say No to Take Control of Your Life. Grand Rapids: Zondervan, 1992.

―――. *False Assumptions: Relief from Twelve "Christian" Beliefs That Can Drive You Crazy.* Grand Rapids: Zondervan, 1994.

Fassel, Diane. *Working Ourselves to Death: The High Cost of Workaholism and the Rewards of Recovery.* San Francisco: HarperCollins, 1990.

Fossum, M. A., and M. J. Mason. *Facing Shame: Families in Recovery.* New York: W. W. Norton, 1986.

Friedman, Edwin H. *Generation to Generation: Family Process in Church and Synagogue.* New York: Guilford, 1985.

Hart, Archibald. *Healing Life's Hidden Addictions.* Ann Arbor: Servant Publications, 1990.

Hemfelt, Robert, Frank Minirth, and Paul Meier. *Love Is a Choice.* Nashville: Thomas Nelson, 1989. Also see the workbook listed below.

Johnson, David, and Jeff VanVonderen. *The Subtle Power of Spiritual Abuse: Recognizing and Escaping Spiritual Manipulation and False Spiritual Authority within the Church.* Minneapolis: Bethany, 1991.

Laaser, M. R. *The Secret Sin: Healing the Wounds of Sexual Addiction.* Grand Rapids: Zondervan, 1992.

May, G. *Addiction and Grace.* New York: Harper and Row, 1988.

McCormick, P. *Sin as Addiction.* Mahwah, N.J.: Paulist, 1989.

McGee, Robert S. *The Search for Significance: We Can Build Our Self-Worth on Our Ability to Please Others, or on the Love and Forgiveness of Jesus Christ.* Houston: Rapha Publishing, 1990. (Book and workbook in one.)

McKay, Matthew, Peter Rogers, and Judith McKay. *When Anger Hurts.* New York: MJF Books, 1989.

Miller, K. *A Hunger for Healing: The Twelve Steps as a Classic Model for Christian Spiritual Growth.* San Francisco: Harper and Row, 1991.

Minirth, Frank, Paul Meier, Siegfried Fink, Walter Byrd, and Don

Hawkins. *Taking Control: New Hope for Substance Abusers and Their Families.* Grand Rapids: Baker, 1988.

Ryan, Dale, and Juanita Ryan. *Rooted in God's Love: Biblical Meditations for People in Recovery.* Downers Grove, Ill.: InterVarsity Press, 1992.

Sloat, D. *Growing Up Holy and Wholly: Understanding and Hope for Adult Children of Evangelicals.* Brentwood, Tenn.: Wolgemuth and Hyatt, 1990.

Smedes, Lewis B. *Shame and Grace: Healing the Shame We Don't Deserve.* San Francisco: HarperCollins, 1993.

———. *Forgive and Forget.* San Francisco: Harper and Row, 1984.

Schaef, Ann Wilson, and Diane Fassel. *The Addictive Organization.* San Francisco: Harper and Row, 1988.

Spickard, Anderson, and Barbara R. Thompson. *Dying for a Drink: What You Should Know about Alcoholism.* Waco, Tex.: Word, 1985.

Twerski, Abraham. *Addictive Thinking: Understanding Self-Deception.* New York: HarperCollins, 1990.

Warren, Neil Clark. *Make Anger Your Ally.* Garden City, N.Y.: Doubleday-Galilee, 1985.

Wegsheider, Sharon. *Another Chance: Hope and Health for the Alcoholic Family.* Palo Alto, Calif.: Science and Recovery Books, 1981.

Westberg, Granger E. *Good Grief.* Philadelphia: Fortress, 1971.

Wilson, Sandra D. *The World According to Me: Recognizing and Releasing Our Illusions of Control.* Wheaton, Ill.: Victor, 1995.

Magazines

STEPS, a quarterly publication of the National Association for Christian Recovery.

Small Group/Individual Recovery Guides

Love Is a Choice Workbook: Recovery for Codependent Relationships. "The doctors of the Minirth-Meier Clinics counsel you

directly using their proven interactive techniques." By Robert
Hemfelt, Frank Minirth, Paul Meier, Deborah Newman, Brian
Newman. Nashville: Thomas Nelson, 1991. Also see the book
by the same name above.
*The Grief Recovery Handbook: A Step-by-Step Program for
Moving Beyond Loss.* By John W. James and Frank Cherry.
New York: Harper and Row, 1988.
The Anger Workbook. By Les Carter and Frank Minirth. Nash-
ville: Thomas Nelson, 1993.
*The Search for Significance: We Can Build Our Self-Worth on Our
Ability to Please Others, or on the Love and Forgiveness of
Jesus Christ.* By Robert S. McGee. Houston: Rapha Publica-
tions, 1990. Book and workbook in one.
Life Recovery Guides. Published by InterVarsity Press, Downers
Grove, IL 60515. Various topics.
Small Group Resources. Various spiritual growth topics, includ-
ing recovery. Serendipity House, P.O. Box 1012, Littleton, CO
80160.

Organizations/Clinics

Alcoholics Anonymous World Services, Inc.
Box 459
Grand Central Station
New York, NY 10163

Minirth-Meier Clinics
For information about a clinic in your area, educational resources,
and hospital programs, call 1-800-545-1819.

National Association for Christian Recovery
P.O. Box 11095
Whittier, CA 90603
1-310-697-6201
1-310-694-6930 (fax)

National Clergy Council on Alcoholism (NCA)
733 Third Avenue
New York, NY 10017

RAPHA: Christ-Centered Hospital and Counseling Care
8876 Gulf Freeway, Suite 340
Houston, TX 77017
1-800-227-2657